The Black Ar

THE GIRL WHO DIED

By Tom Marshall

Published April 2023 by Obverse Books

Editors: Philip Purser-Hallard, Paul Driscoll

For Joanna, min älskling, or 'The Girl Who Patiently Endured Me Working On This Project'

and

in memory of Neil Hadfield, finest of English teachers.

Recently Published

#52: *The Battle of Ranskoor Av Kolos* by James McGrath
#53: *The Hand of Fear* by Simon Bucher-Jones
#54: *Dalek* by Billy Seguire
#55: *Invasion of the Dinosaurs* by Jon Arnold
#56: *The Haunting of Villa Diodati* by Philip Purser-Hallard
#57: *Vincent and the Doctor* by Paul Driscoll
#58: *The Talons of Weng-Chiang* by Dale Smith
#59: *Kill the Moon* by Darren Mooney
#60: *The Sun Makers* by Lewis Baston
#61: *Paradise Towers* by John Toon
#62: *Kinda* by Frank Collins
#63: *Flux* edited by Paul Driscoll

CONTENTS

OVERVIEW

Serial Title: *The Girl Who Died*

Writer: Jamie Mathieson and Steven Moffat

Director: Ed Bazalgette

Original UK Transmission Dates: 17 October 2015

Running Time: 45m 41s

UK Viewing Figures: 6.56 million

Regular Cast: Peter Capaldi (the Doctor), Jenna Coleman (Clara)[1]

Guest Cast: Maisie Williams (Ashildr), David Schofield (Odin), Simon Lipkin (Nollar), Ian Conningham (Chuckles), Tom Stourton (Lofty), Alastair Parker (Limpy), Murray McArthur (Hasten), Barnaby Kay (Heidi)

Antagonists: 'Odin', the Mire

Responses:

'Certainly, **Doctor Who**'s unique format allows it to transcend genres. However, unlike, say *Love and Monsters*, which paired absurdist humour and melancholy to portray the isolation of early adulthood, *The Girl Who Died* incorporates so many disparate tone shifts as to suffer from identity crisis.'

[Clint Hassell, *Doctor Who TV*]

---

[1] David Tennant and Catherine Tate appear uncredited as the 10th Doctor and Donna in footage from *The Fires of Pompeii* (2008), in which Capaldi also appears as Caecilius.

'*The Girl Who Died* is a damn triumph. More than that, it's a triumph because it feels so resolutely like a **Doctor Who** episode [...] all the pieces – the writing, the acting, the directing – combine to create what is quite possibly the best episode yet of this Doctor's tenure.'

[Alasdair Wilkins, *AV Club*]

SYNOPSIS

Narrowly surviving a space battle, **the Doctor** and a spacesuited **Clara** arrive on Earth, where they are captured by Vikings led by **Hasten**. Their captors separate them from the TARDIS, break the Doctor's sonic sunglasses and take them in chains to their village, where they meet an unusual young woman – **Ashildr**, daughter of **Einarr**. The Doctor attempts to pose as the Norse god Odin, but is interrupted by the appearance in the sky of a far more convincing pretender.

This **'Odin'** promises that the village's best warriors will feast with him in Valhalla, and sends down armoured soldiers to collect them. When Clara tries to persuade Ashildr to use the Doctor's broken sunglasses to free her, the aliens detect that both women carry advanced technology, and they too are transported to their spaceship. There they see Hasten, **Nollar** and the other warriors killed, and their hormones harvested to stimulate the aliens. Clara nearly persuades 'Odin' to leave, but instead a furious Ashildr declares war on the aliens. 'Odin' accepts her challenge and returns the women to the village, giving them a day to prepare for battle.

The Doctor has identified the aliens as **the Mire**, a deadly warrior race. He urges the villagers – now without their warriors – to run, but honour compels them to stay and fight. Ashildr and Clara plead with the Doctor to help, but he insists on his duty not to interfere in the past. However, when he hears a baby (whose crying he is able to translate) referring to 'fire in the water', he reluctantly agrees.

He first makes an effort to drill the village men, whom he nicknames 'Chuckles', **'Lofty'**, **'Limpy'** and **'Heidi'** (Chuckles being

Ashildr's father Einarr), as fighters, but this is a failure. The Doctor then puts together a complex plan involving the villagers' captive electric eels, the wiring from Clara's spacesuit and a dragon puppet created by Ashildr, an inveterate storyteller. When the Mire warriors and 'Odin' arrive, they are assailed by electricity and a magnetised anvil. The latter allows the Doctor to purloin a Mire helmet, into which he plugs Ashildr. From there she can use her visionary storytelling to make the Mire perceive the puppet as a real dragon, causing all except 'Odin' to retreat. The Doctor threatens to make their defeat public, destroying the Mire's reputation, and the aliens leave, humiliated. However, the strain has proven too much for Ashildr's heart and she dies, to Einarr's great distress.

Distraught and sick of his own immortality, the Doctor rails against the code of conduct that prevents him from doing anything to save her. However, a sight of his reflection reminds him that his current face was copied from a Pompeiian man, **Caecilius**, whose family he rescued from the eruption of Vesuvius, and he is inspired once again to intervene. He reprograms a Mire battlefield medical kit to repair Ashildr, not only resurrecting her, but rendering her incapable of dying. Knowing what it is to lose others to death, he gives her a second device that she can use on a companion if she chooses. The Doctor leaves, launching a new immortal upon the universe.

NOTES ON TERMINOLOGY

A distinction must be drawn between 'Old Norse' and 'Old Norse-Icelandic'. The former refers to the **language** that was spoken by the inhabitants of medieval Scandinavia and in which the mythological sources are written. The latter adjective, for political reasons connected with Icelandic national identity and the origin of the sagas, is applied to the body of **literature** written in that language; it is common to read of '(Old) Norse literature' in the public sphere, but the term is not current academic parlance and as such will not be used.

This book makes frequent reference to the deity both the Doctor and the leader of the Mire pose as, who will be referred to in the following ways:

a. In accordance with Norse studies, the Old Norse spelling **Óðinn** is used here when referring to the figure of myth outside of **Doctor Who**.
b. The popular Anglicisation **Odin** refers to the god who is namechecked in the TV story, but does not appear.
c. **'Odin'** refers to the leader of the Mire we see adopting the identity of b. within the fiction.

The adjective **Odinic** will also be used throughout; it is a 19th-century academic coining and has no Old Norse equivalent.

Other Norse characters and terms, or Viking names, will generally follow Old Norse orthography except for names specific to *The Girl Who Died*: e.g., the eponymous character is **Ashildr**, not the more linguistically accurate Áshildr.

Speaking of whom, she will be referred to as 'Ashildr' throughout for the sake of clarity, rather than the name 'Me' which she later adopts for herself – even when discussing her appearances in subsequent episodes.

INTRODUCTION

Perhaps the best place to begin is before the beginning. Prior to being christened *The Girl Who Died*, Jamie Mathieson's episode of **Doctor Who** for the 2015 season had the working title 'The Allfather's Army'[2]. These three words are an inspired encapsulation of the two different and seemingly contradictory modes in which the episode operates, reflecting in microcosm the ideological battle at the story's heart. This might seem something of a grandiose claim, so it is worth unpacking.

As many readers will know, the moniker 'All-Father' (i.e., Father-of-Everything, from the Old Norse 'Alfǫðr') is commonly used to describe the prominent Norse god Óðinn. This makes the working title a Norse-flavoured pun on the classic British sitcom **Dad's Army** (1968-77), with the hapless Viking warriors evoking that programme's comically inept Home Guard during the Second World War. On the one hand, then, *The Girl Who Died* draws on Norse mythology and medievalist trappings, familiar to mass audiences from such film and television successes as the **Lord of the Rings** trilogy (2001-03), **Game of Thrones** (2011-19), and **Vikings** (2013-20). On the other, it is indebted to a distinctly, irreverently British sensibility of slapstick, farce, and general silliness to be found in programmes such as **Dad's Army** and **Monty Python's Flying Circus** (1969-74). The final result is a blend of these two major influences.

---

[2] *Doctor Who: The Complete History* (TCH) Volume 81, p87. It was renamed so as to better 'twin' it with the following episode, *The Woman Who Lived* (2015), and fit in with the season's pattern of twinned titles.

These very distinct aspects may not seem like a particularly intuitive fit, and that apparently jarring awkwardness may have generated some of the more lukewarm responses to the story. Largely, of course, this is a feature rather than a bug, the clashing contrast between relatively serious medieval grit and more laidback knockabout humour being the point of the exercise. But the blend of the two is a defter and more natural one than it might first appear. Indeed, they go hand-in-hand in certain sagas and poems in the traditions of Norse-Icelandic literature itself, and thus there is even a kind of fidelity to Norse culture in such an outlandish juxtaposition. The story is particularly adept at shifting between these different registers, especially within the episode's second half, in which proceedings move seamlessly from comic to tragic, ridiculous to sublime.

The interplay between these two registers (sometimes discordant, sometimes harmonious) is the predominant subject of the rest of this book. Each chapter examines how *The Girl Who Died* – one of the most quietly radical **Who** stories of all – challenges conventional wisdom and popular assumptions about Vikings and Norse society, the importance of historical accuracy, whether it is safe to trust one's own eyes, the rigid boundaries of traditional gender roles, and what types of stories are worth telling.

Chapter 1 examines how the story deviates from the typical popular culture take on Vikings and assumptions about both heroic masculinity and history itself. Chapter 2 looks at the story's championing of playful, irreverent humour in the face of toxic masculinity, especially in the context of the modern-day far right's unhealthy obsession with Vikings. Chapter 3 delves into the multiple ways in which the Doctor and the mythological Óðinn resemble each other, and to what extent this illuminates the former's depiction here as a healer-trickster. Chapter 4 deals with the titular 'girl', Ashildr, and particularly with the way her transgressive gender identity contributes to the story's queer subtext. Finally, the concluding chapter draws these strands together in an analysis of the episode's denouement: not only the means by which the alien threat is defeated, but also the Doctor's morally complex act of resurrecting Ashildr.

Key to my argument throughout this book will be two concepts drawn from medieval literature – **apotropaic laughter** and **soteriological trickery** – both of which may require a brief explanation here. If something is apotropaic, it has the capacity to ward off evil, while something which is soteriological essentially offers salvation – usually in the religious sense, although here being used in a more secular capacity. Both terms circle back to that same blend of the supernatural, the mythological, the cosmically significant, with the comedic, the playful, and the downright silly.

CHAPTER 1: A DEADLY (SERIOUS) WARRIOR RACE

1.1: 'Not Vikings, I'm Not in the Mood for Vikings'[3]

A thousand years or so ago, the Scandinavian raiders known as Vikings were everywhere, travelling to locations as diverse as Greenland, North Africa, Russia, Baghdad, and Newfoundland[4]. In the 21st century, their reach is equally extensive, but instead of conquering land they are conquering space in popular culture and the public imagination. The trend for depicting Vikings or drawing on Old Norse-Icelandic literature is not uniquely modern but can be traced back across centuries of literary tradition; the debt Western literature owes to Norse influence has been described as 'immeasurable'[5]. From William Blake to Seamus Heaney, from Thomas Hardy to WH Auden, from Robert Louis Stevenson to JRR Tolkien, something about the wild and pillaging Northmen of sagas and poems has captivated and inspired many writers traditionally included within the literary 'canon', across multiple media and genres[6].

---

[3] All quotations taken from *The Girl Who Died* unless otherwise stated.

[4] See e.g., Jarman, Cat, *River Kings: The Vikings from Scandinavia to the Silk Roads*; and Magnus Magnusson and Hermann Pálsson, trans, *The Vinland Sagas: The Norse Discovery of America*.

[5] O'Donoghue, Heather, *Old Norse-Icelandic Literature: A Short Introduction*, p149.

[6] For a useful survey of Norse influence on these figures, see O'Donoghue, *Old Norse-Icelandic Literature,* pp149-201.

This fascination has far from died out in the age of film, television, and video games – quite the opposite. Depictions of Viking warriors can be found in a range of imaginatively titled films across the decades, such as *The Viking* (1928), *The Vikings* (1958), *The Norseman* (1978), and *The Northman* (2022). If anything, TV series have made even more mileage out of the historical period, especially with the success of recent programmes such as **Vikings** and its sequel series **Vikings: Valhalla** (2022), alongside other examples including **The Last Kingdom** (2015-22). Most of the above purport to (at least semi-seriously) depict historical Vikings, but, perhaps more relevantly for **Doctor Who**, the influence can also be widely felt across the fantasy genre.

Tolkien, a professor of Old English, drew extensively on his knowledge of Norse-Icelandic texts in creating the world of Middle-Earth and writing *The Hobbit* (1937) and **The Lord of the Rings** (1954-55), right down to openly borrowing names from the 10th-century poem *Vǫluspá* for major characters[7]. These books remain high-profile and much-loved, in part thanks to their 2001-03 and 2012-14 film adaptation trilogies, and the TV series **The Lord of the Rings: The Rings of Power** (2022-). Other works of epic fantasy, such as George RR Martin's **A Song of Ice and Fire** (1996-), draw less obviously on Norse mythology; nonetheless, studies have examined the use of Nordic motifs in both the books and their TV

---

[7] O'Donoghue, *Old Norse-Icelandic Literature*, p155; *Vǫluspá*, stanzas 10-16 (Larrington, Carolyne, trans, *The Poetic Edda*, pp5-6). See also Fimi, Dimitra, 'Tolkien and Old Norse Antiquity: Real and Romantic Links in Material Culture', in Clark, David and Carl Phelpstead, eds, *Old Norse Made New*, pp83-99.

adaptation, **Game of Thrones**[8]. Not to be outdone, Marvel Comics' **Thor** titles – reimagining the Norse gods as a science-fiction civilisation – began in 1962, with Chris Hemsworth's on-screen portrayal of the title character having appeared in nine films and one animated TV series since 2011.

Doctor Who itself has been no stranger to borrowing from Norse-Icelandic literature, either: perhaps most obviously in *The Time Meddler* (1965), depicting Vikings arriving on the Northumbrian coast in 1066, but also drawing on Norse mythology and iconography in stories such as *Terminus* (1983), *The Greatest Show in the Galaxy* (1988-89), and *The Curse of Fenric* (1989). Still, it is perhaps surprising that, by 2015, only one televised story out of around 250 had actually shown Vikings on screen, and 50 years ago at that[9]. Executive producer Steven Moffat's brief (to writer Jamie Mathieson) of a story he had always wanted to do – 'the Doctor meets Vikings'[10] – should therefore be viewed within this context: as modern **Doctor Who**'s attempt to definitively 'do a Viking story' against a backdrop of many other film and TV versions[11].

---

[8] See especially Larrington, Carolyne, *Winter is Coming: The Medieval World of Game of Thrones*.

[9] The 'space Viking' character of Gantok in *The Wedding of River Song* (2011) seems a borderline case, and as such is discounted here.

[10] TCH #81, p86.

[11] Notably, *The Girl Who Died* shares a number of key personnel with **The Last Kingdom** (2015-22) – namely, Ed Bazalgette (the latter series' most prolific director, with six episodes and the series feature film, *Seven Kings Must Die* (2023), to his name, as well as being a co-executive producer) and actors David Schofield and Ian Conningham. Their work on **Who** would not have guaranteed

Unsurprisingly, the **Doctor Who** take on 'a Viking story' ends up rather at odds with most wider pop culture examples. Partly, this can be put down to the presence of such **Doctor Who** staples as spaceships and alien invaders, although the more supernatural aspects of Norse mythology do not have to be contorted too much to take on a science-fiction veneer[12]. Partly, it can be explained by the status of **Who** as a family show watched by children, in stark contrast to most successful 21st-century TV programmes about Vikings, which are quick to pile on 'realistic' levels of gore and sexual assault. Clearly, it would not be suitable for **Who** to depict such adult content.

Of greatest interest, however, is a third way in which *The Girl Who Died* differs from other conventional depictions of Vikings; namely, the way it sets out to directly challenge, problematise, and indeed make fun of wider pop culture assumptions about who the Vikings were and how they behaved. To understand how it goes about doing this, those assumptions will first need to be outlined.

For a crystal-clear expression of how the masculine Viking warrior role is commonly viewed, we need look no further than the opening episode of the first season of **Vikings**:

---

involvement with **The Last Kingdom**, but past form with televised medievalism and Vikings would surely not have hurt. Similarly, Murray McArthur has gone on to play other fierce Northmen in **Game of Thrones** (2011-19) and *The Northman* (2022).

[12] As noted above, this ground has already been covered by the **Thor** franchise; additionally, the video game *The Lost Vikings* (1993) involves both aliens and time travel, while **Stargate SG-1** (1997-2007) reimagines 'the Asgard' as an alien race.

RAGNAR LOTHBROK

What does a man do?

BJÖRN

He fights.[13]

This is a blunt and reductive summary within a fictitious conversation. Nonetheless, it succinctly and accurately gets to the heart of the pop culture understanding of (male) Vikings, who are invariably perceived – and in many cases admired – for their brutal and stoic masculinity. Stereotypical hyper-masculine Viking traits include a propensity for bloody violence, a love of adventure and conquest, coarse and brash behaviour, and an almost unquenchable appetite for food, drink, and women[14]. As Neil Price puts it:

> 'ask anyone about the Vikings today, and most will instantly summon an image of longships coursing the seas, decks crowded with long-haired, muscled warriors on their way to plunder and burn [...] the scene is resolutely maritime, violent – and male, to the extent that the Vikings have become almost a caricature of masculinity.'[15]

This exaggerated hyper-masculinity, with its hardiness, ferocity, and a determination to die with honour, is no doubt at the heart of the Vikings' extraordinarily persistent popularity. It is also an oversimplification – much like the simplification of the word

[13] **Vikings**: *Rite of Passage* (2013).
[14] Trafford, Simon, 'Hyper-Masculinity vs Viking warrior-Women: Pop Culture Vikings and Gender'.
[15] Price, Neil, 'Unpacking the Viking Caricature of Masculinity'.

'Viking' itself, which strictly speaking referred not to an ethnic identity but those who participated in a specific activity. A 'vikingr' was a raider who went abroad on expeditions[16]. Lurid imagery of violent attacks by pillaging pirates does not give us the full picture of masculinity in medieval Scandinavia, ignoring farmers and landowners, elderly men, thralls and slaves, shamans, and indeed the sick and differently abled[17]. Nor does it account for the ways that the patriarchal structures of such societies could be undermined even by subversive customs that were part of that structure (which will be explored more fully in the discussion of Viking women)[18].

Nevertheless, it is this particular perception of Vikings that has endured and entrenched itself in popular culture. The vast majority of televisual media depicting Norsemen which was surveyed as background research for this book hews close to this familiar template. There are often warrior women alongside the men,

---

[16] For this reason, some scholars prefer the uncapitalised 'viking' and use it to refer exclusively to the activity rather than to Scandinavian peoples (see Cooijmans, Christian, 'Beyond Hostility and Hypermasculinity: Why We Need to Think Differently About the Vikings'), while others have argued that the word should be abandoned altogether (Woolf, Alex, 'Goodbye to the Vikings'). The conventional, if erroneous, ethnic identity usage (instead of 'Norse') is broadly retained in this book for the purposes of clarity and reader familiarity; this is also the usage found in the episode, e.g., in Einarr's declaration that he and the other non-raider villagers 'are Vikings!'

[17] Price, 'Unpacking the Viking Caricature'.

[18] Price, Neil, 'What Stereotypes About Viking Masculinity Get Wrong'.

granted, but this too is part of an old literary tradition and is not always to the credit of such media. For the most part, Viking warriors are consistently portrayed in all the ways one would expect – tall, muscular, (often) blond-haired and blue-eyed, brutally violent, and utterly insatiable when it comes to satisfying their physical needs. Many are costumed in almost biker-gang-style leather and horned helmets – both glaringly anachronistic details which have become key parts of the popular imagination, for better or for worse.

If the reader were to select one of the many Viking-themed films or television programmes mentioned in the bibliography, they would likely encounter gritty, mud-spattered battle sequences, with chaotic and grisly action conveyed in dramatic slow motion for extra impact; be subjected to the raucous noise of war cries and the rousing clang of axes on shields; and hear at least one conversation about meeting death with honour so as to attain a place in the feasting-hall afterlife of Valhǫll (Valhalla). These depictions would appear to be based on the assumption that the more brutal the violence, the bloodier the slaughter, and the grittier the milieu, the more likely it is that a film or TV series will be praised for its 'realism', its unflinching honesty, and the sense that it depicts a medieval (or medieval-inspired) world 'as it was really like'. Even in **Doctor Who**'s one previous engagement with Vikings – *The Time Meddler* – the story's strong vein of outright comedy is focussed on the eponymous meddler, not on the marauding Scandinavians. They may get occasionally outwitted, but are still played comparatively straight, as a force to be feared, rather than something that should be joked about[19].

It should be stressed here that such 'realistic', relatively unreconstructed depictions are not inherently bad. The distance between the Viking Age[20] and our own, coupled with the fact that there is still a significant amount we do not know, rather discredits the idea that any such depiction, even Robert Eggers' much-vaunted *The Northman*, can truly attain 'historical accuracy'. Nonetheless, there is certainly something to be said for serious efforts to portray historical periods warts and all, without sanitising them. In many cases, however, a refusal to sanitise ugly truths leads to other problems. What can end up being created is an excessive aesthetic of glorifying barbaric violence; over-zealously prioritising shocking and bloodthirsty 'twists' in the hope of getting the audience talking; and tackling sensitive and traumatic topics without the care and sensitivity they deserve, especially graphic sexual assault. By leaning heavily into depictions of violence and brutality, and by focussing almost exclusively on warriorhood or revenge narratives, even better-received films and TV series can elide the diversity of roles played during the Viking Age, from farmers and priests to merchants and diplomats. Just as early medieval Christian sources may well have exaggerated the Vikings' propensity for violence to suit their own agenda, this simplified approach typecasts Vikings as rampaging, barbarous berserkers,

---

[19] This creates something of a jarring tone between the overall light-heartedness of the piece and the rather sombre (but brief) moment in which it is implied that Edith, one of the Saxons, has been raped by the Vikings.

[20] Typically defined as lasting from 793 to 1066 CE, the period of the Norsemen's major raiding and conquests.

even in films which unambiguously depict them as horrifying. In doing so, it unwittingly arms modern-day white supremacists with significant ammunition for their own distorted understanding of the Viking Age[21].

There is, however, a second tradition running in parallel alongside these more serious-minded portrayals, one which merrily pokes fun at the usual understanding of the Vikings. Prominent examples include the children's TV serial **Noggin the Nog** (1959-65, 1982), the film *Erik the Viking* (1989), Taika Waititi's two *Thor* films, and the Norwegian sitcom **Norsemen** (2016-20). The first of these, meant for young children, presents its titular character as fundamentally good-hearted, soft-voiced, and kindly – essentially a 'thoroughly decent sort of chap' British archetype clothed in the unlikely garb of a Viking warrior[22]. In *Erik the Viking*, the central joke is that the mild-mannered Erik has far too much of a conscience to be successful at all the raping and pillaging that is expected of him, while gods such as Óðinn and Þórr (Thor) are portrayed as petulant children rather than figures to inspire awe. Both Noggin and Erik ultimately pull through their various adventures with their dignity intact, rather the better off for avoiding the excesses of hyper-masculinity.

Thor: Ragnarok (2017) and *Thor: Love and Thunder* (2022) are particularly happy to play up various 'Norse god' characters for laughs, with the eponymous, heavily muscled warrior-god frequently ending up the butt of the joke himself. **Norsemen** does

---

[21] Cooijmans, 'Beyond Hostility and Hypermasculinity'.
[22] In an ad lib by Peter Capaldi (TCH #81, p109), the Doctor names one of his trainee warriors after Noggin in *The Girl Who Died*.

not shy away from the grim reality of the Viking world – its brutal physical and sexual violence – but finds humour in the inadequacy and insecurities of many of the lead characters. There is also a side order of jet-black schadenfreude as certain individuals' attempts to be (anachronistically) modern and forward-thinking only land them, rather bleakly and mean-spiritedly, in direr straits. Even certain Old Norse sources themselves seem to mock hyper-masculine ideals. The rogue Vilhjálmr in *Göngu-Hrólfs Saga* is depicted as desperately, comically insecure with regard to his own masculinity, such as in his excessive boasts of his courage and strength and in his declaration that he is a paragon of manliness. Eventually, of course, he is found out[23].

Similarly, *The Girl Who Died* goes to considerable lengths to subvert expectations about the sort of hyper-masculinity generally associated with 'a Viking story' or indeed with most stories drawing on medieval warfare. Take the episode's rather disdainful treatment of its macho warrior characters – the sort who are frequently the focus of so many other depictions of Vikings. Early on, it feints at the idea that these hyper-masculine warriors will take centre stage here, too: they are the first guest characters we encounter, in the story's pre-title sequence no less, and they are not initially comedic. Indeed, they rather get the better of the Doctor. He boasts of his own technological superiority over medieval humans in the form of his sonic sunglasses, but these are

---

[23] Hermann Pálsson and Paul Edwards, ed and trans, *Göngu-Hrolf's Saga: A Viking Romance*, pp53-68. See also Lavender, Philip, 'Vulnerable Masculinities and the Vicissitudes of Power in *Göngu-Hrólfs Saga*' in Evans, Gareth Lloyd, and Jessica Clare Hancock, eds, *Masculinities in Old Norse Literature*, pp100-03.

promptly removed and snapped in two by Hasten, leader of the raiding party, leading the Doctor to sheepishly acquiesce to going wherever these Viking overlords take them. Far from being comic foils, they have swiftly bested the Time Lord by destroying (the current form of) his all-purpose, plot-resolving, get-out-of-jail-free tool[24]. In more ways than one, the story starts out in an 'almost aggressively traditional' vein[25].

Once the title sequence has rolled, however, it is a different matter altogether, as though entering the tenuous reality of a **Doctor Who** story proper has stripped the Vikings of their ferocity as well as their formerly impressive grip on the narrative. Striding back into his home village, Hasten now sports one broken half of the Doctor's sonic sunglasses on his face – no doubt in imitation of Óðinn's eyepatch, but also a rather ridiculous-looking anachronism that serves to diminish the character and make him hard to take seriously any more. His response to being asked whether all the raiders have returned – 'I suppose so, I haven't counted' – is deliberately exaggerated, as if in parody of legendary Viking gruffness and stoicism.

The arrival of the Mire – essentially, bigger and 'badder' Vikings than the Vikings themselves – upstages and minimises these warriors further. Having been selected by the Mire as the fittest and the strongest, Hasten and the others are unceremoniously

---

[24] This is a signature trope of Jamie Mathieson's – he similarly destroys the sonic screwdriver early into *Oxygen* (2017) and, as here, renders the TARDIS inaccessible or non-operational in *Mummy on the Orient Express* and *Flatline* (both 2014).

[25] Mooney, Darren, '**Doctor Who**: *The Girl Who Died* (Review)'.

offed with a soupçon of black humour. Promptly after boasting 'there's nothing to fear, strange maiden – we are Odin's chosen!' and ignoring Clara's warnings, Hasten is disintegrated, leaving behind only a rather pathetic-looking horned helmet. The others quickly follow suit, having failed to stop a moving wall from pushing them into the path of the lethal energy discharge, and not having been smart enough to try opening the door at the other end of the room like Clara and Ashildr[26]. Imagining they have already arrived in their beloved Valhalla where they will feast with the father of the gods, these warriors die in a blind panic, tricked by an imposter and devoid of the battlefield honour they crave. This is followed by the Mire leader's bleak punchline ('what is a god but the cattle's name for farmer? What is heaven but the gilded door of the abattoir?'), which nicely sums up the futility of their worship. Their chosen deity never once showed up, except to herd them into a pen and slaughter them. So much for the idols of hyper-masculinity.

1.2: 'You Mash up Vikings to Make Warrior Juice, Nice'

As already mentioned, the role the Mire play in *The Girl Who Died* is to fundamentally one-up the Vikings by taking their major characteristics and heavily exaggerating them. On one level, this serves to make them a more formidable threat, quickly unseating the Vikings as antagonists – they are literally bigger and more imposing; their armoured suits are of sturdy metal; their laser guns

---

[26] Arguably an echo of *The Day of the Doctor* (2013), in which Clara thinks to try an unlocked jail cell door but the three Doctors in the cell do not.

clearly outmatch swords and shields; and their weapon forges are so loud and intimidating they can be mistaken for thunder. More to the point, the Mire swiftly establish their martial superiority by wiping out the village's best warriors in one fell swoop. Their modus operandi resembles typical raider behaviour in many ways: invaders who rampage into homesteads, 'get what they want and go', leaving devastation in their wake. Subjected to the ruthless excesses of an even greater warrior race, the Vikings themselves become mere 'cattle', a local resource to be exploited and profited from, much like the acquisitions they seize on their own raids. This is an approach science fiction has been taking ever since imperialist 19th-century Britain was first subjected to invasion by the Martians[27].

However, for much of the episode the Mire are treated no less irreverently and mockingly than the Vikings. The critique the story is making of toxic masculinity targets both groups, juxtaposing the Vikings with an even more exaggerated version of their own behaviour. In this way, this kind of macho posturing is inflated to ludicrous proportions in order to highlight just how laughable it fundamentally is – taking the classic satirical approach of 'exaggerated lunacy'[28].

This manifests in multiple forms, from the over-the-top nature of

---

[27] Wells, HG, *The War of the Worlds*. The comparison was made explicit in dialogue cut from the episode, as the Doctor would have observed that the Vikings might look like gods to those whose villagers **they** raided (TCH #81, p102).

[28] O'Day, Andrew, 'Towards a Definition of Satire in *Doctor Who*', in Hansen, Christopher J, ed, *Ruminations, Peregrinations and Regenerations: A Critical Approach to Doctor Who*, p265.

their stomping legs and comically impractical, clanking armour to the fact that underneath their colossal helmets they look like lampreys[29]. But perhaps the most amusing is the idea that the Mire collect essence of testosterone and adrenaline distilled from mushed Viking warriors, which they loudly proclaim to be 'nectar'. This 'warrior juice' mirrors the real-world phenomenon of taking anabolic steroids, including testosterone, for the purposes of building muscle and enhancing performance in the world of sport. The majority of users are not competitive athletes, however, but instead seek cosmetic 'improvements', i.e., they want to look more masculine[30].

More broadly, the pseudoscientific modern conception of 'alpha' (dominant or conventionally masculine) and 'beta' (insufficiently assertive) males – terms from the animal kingdom crudely applied to humans – is mirrored by the Vikings' culture of hegemonic masculinity[31]. The phrase refers to 'a dominant form of masculinity

---

[29] Jack Graham observes the Mire's resemblance to these toothed fish in 'A Surfeit of Lampreys'. Although lampreys are not related to eels, they are certainly eel-like in body shape and are sometimes referred to as 'lamprey eels'. Electric eels – which also appear in this story – are not properly speaking eels either, making the two an appropriate fit. There is also something amusingly appropriate about humble electric eels aiding in the defeat of supersized militaristic lampreys from space.

[30] Reuters Health, 'Most Steroid Users Are Not Athletes: Study'. It should of course be noted that there are plenty of valid medical reasons for taking steroidal androgens such as testosterone, including as part of masculinising hormone therapy for trans men or intersex individuals.

[31] Raffield, Ben, 'Playing Vikings: Militarism, Hegemonic Masculinities, and Childhood Enculturation in Viking Age

that many individuals strive toward but only a few attain,'[32] creating a hierarchy which positions conventional masculinity as innately superior to more nonconformist or subversive forms, those closer to archetypal femininity. Such a societal model promotes competition and a desire to discredit others: if you feel threatened with regard to your own rung on the ladder, you can always denigrate or belittle the manhood of others to draw attention away from your own inadequacies or increase your own standing within the pecking order.

It is unsurprising, then, that boasting contests or 'mannjafnaðir' (literally 'comparisons of men') appear multiple times in Norse-Icelandic literature[33], as does the practice of insulting another's manhood or honour (known as a flyting, or 'senna'), often through one of the twin prejudices of misogyny or homophobia[34]. Characters in multiple Old Norse poems and sagas either insinuate or state outright that an opponent engages in sexual deviancy of some sort or is insufficiently manly; 'you act more like a woman than a grown man'[35] is a typical such insult. Such accusations could bring the social stigma of 'níð' (dishonour, cowardice, and implied

---

Scandinavia', *Current Anthropology* 60:6, pp818-21. See also Connell, Raewyn, *Masculinities*, where the term originates.

[32] Raffield, 'Playing Vikings', p818.

[33] See, e.g., *Morkinskinna* (Andersson, Theodore M, and Kari Ellen Gade, trans, pp345-7) and *Örvar-Odds saga* (in Hermann Pálsson and Paul Edwards, ed and trans, *Seven Viking Romances*, pp101-08).

[34] Examples include *Hárbarðsljóð*, *Lokasenna*, and *Helgakviða Hundingsbana I* (Larrington, *The Poetic Edda*, pp65-73, 80-92, and 110-18).

[35] Pálsson and Edwards, *Göngu-Hrolf's Saga*, p37.

effeminacy or homosexuality) – which was taken seriously enough to warrant being enshrined in the law codes of the day[36].

While it would be pretty tasteless, in a modern context, to have a hero taunt a villain for being gay or effeminate, **Doctor Who** has long made use of scenes of heroic characters making fun of villainous ones, and *The Girl Who Died* is no exception. The extent to which this successfully comes off varies – Clara's quip to the Mire leader, 'time for your medication?', is meant to skewer her opponent's assumed alpha masculinity by pointing out his reliance on a stimulant or drug, but arguably perpetuates the ableist stereotype that relying on medication is a weakness. In one draft, the Mire leader would have been revealed as a 'tiny, helpless alien'[37], exposing how fundamentally small he is despite a desire to seem intimidating and impressive, although again equating power and strength with physical size (or the respective lack thereof) might perhaps not have been the best idea.

More successful is the highlighting of the fundamental insecurity at the heart of the Mire's strutting, testosterone-enhanced displays of belligerence. As with Vilhjálmr in *Göngu-Hrólfs saga*, the Mire's excessive boasting (e.g., 'I have no reason to fear you', 'talk is for cowards', 'war is our way') is a mask for their own weaknesses. Their supposed machismo or bravado is rather undercut by the fact that they are provoked by the taunts of a young girl into fighting a village of 'farmers and fishermen' (the polar opposite of picking on someone their own size). Additionally, far from upholding some sort of honour code, they have been perfectly happy to 'open fire

---

[36] O'Donoghue, *Old Norse-Icelandic Literature*, pp31-32.
[37] TCH #81, p90.

on unarmed civilians' in the past, if their leader's comments are any indication.

It soon becomes clear that the Mire's reputation as 'one of the deadliest warrior races in the galaxy' and 'brutal, sadistic, undefeated' is just that – a reputation, an embellished narrative rather than the truth. When faced with a fearsome-looking beast which seems impervious to their firepower, the Mire soldiers swiftly teleport away, prompting jeers of 'Cowards!' even from their leader. This is made doubly embarrassing by the comic video taken of the humiliating defeat and the fact that the fearsome-looking beast is actually a not terribly convincing wooden puppet. As the Doctor points out, their public image as a mighty force could unravel entirely: 'Even I believed the stories. But after today, no one will again. An army like yours, it lives or dies on its reputation, its story'. The risk of the footage being uploaded to 'the galactic hub' – effectively, an outer-space YouTube – and the irreparable damage this exposure would do to their macho reputation is enough to send the Mire packing. This modern version of the senna is the perfect conclusion to the episode's gleeful pastiche of hyper-masculinity: they have been thoroughly knocked off their perch within their beloved hegemony.

1.3: 'That's Probably a Viking Saying, I Haven't Checked That'

At first glance, the question of to what extent (if any!) *The Girl Who Died* is historically accurate in its depiction of Norway circa 850 CE[38]

[38] No date is given on screen. *The Woman Who Lived* (set in 1651) makes it clear that '800 years' have passed for Ashildr. She is

might seem unconnected to its satirical depiction of the hyper-masculinity of both the Vikings and the Mire. In first showing up the manliest Viking warriors and then the even-more-manliest Mire warriors, however, the story's tone – in this aspect at least – is firmly ironic and bathetic. Without making any declarative statements, it invites the audience to consider the possibility that Vikings were **not** unanimously powerful, savage, and terrifying – and indeed that insisting on that sort of unreconstructed, conventional view is faintly ridiculous. In short, this amounts to taking a stance on how we perceive Viking history.

When engaging with the past, **Doctor Who** frequently (though by no means exclusively) employs a relatively uncritical approach dubbed 'heritage theme-park history'[39], embracing stock, familiar tropes as a kind of narrative shorthand. History is presented the way people popularly remember it, as quaint picture-postcard period drama with as few challenging wrinkles as possible: Churchill as plucky wartime leader, Victorian Britain as twinkling and twee, a hotchpotch of generic Middle Ages motifs[40]. Anything

---

presumably rounding down slightly, as 850 is the year given by both the photo novelisation (Rollason, Jane, *Doctor Who: The Girl Who Died*, p1) and by Lance Parkin and Lars Pearson in *AHistory: An Unauthorized History of the Doctor Who Universe (Fourth Edition Vol 1)*, p1095. It is also not specified that the story is set in Norway, but that seems likeliest based on the mountainous terrain and the origin of many of the ninth-century raiders.

[39] Sandifer, Elizabeth, *TARDIS Eruditorum: An Unofficial Critical History of Doctor Who Volume 6: Peter Davison & Colin Baker*, p201; Miles, Lawrence, and Tat Wood, *About Time 5: The Unauthorized Guide to Doctor Who – Seasons 18 to 21*, p230.

[40] In *Victory of the Daleks* (2010), various episodes from *The*

too prickly and complicated is ignored, either because of writers' ignorance of, or disinterest in, such issues; or a (frankly, misguided) assumption that 'political' subject matter is inappropriate for children; or because of the understandable constraints of running time holding back a deeper exploration of the topic. Such stories are very much set in the 'histories of the common imagination'[41].

In some respects, *The Girl Who Died* does embrace 'theme park history', going along with popular but inaccurate perceptions of the Vikings because they make for an easy visual shorthand in terms of communicating with the audience. A major example is the production design choice to use stereotypical horned helmets, despite Mathieson being fully aware of the historical inaccuracy:

> 'you realise you have to go with a sort of collective view of what Vikings were like. For example, the actual Vikings of history didn't have horns on their helmets. But the **Doctor Who** version has to. Of course they do! Because if you don't, then they don't look like what everyone expects of Vikings'.[42]

Although the image of Vikings wearing horned helmets is in fact an invention stemming from an 1876 staging of Richard Wagner's opera cycle *Der Ring des Nibelungen* (1848-74), the story would

---

Unquiet Dead (2005) onwards, and *The King's Demons* (1983).

[41] O'Mahony, Daniel, '"Now How is That Wolf Able to Impersonate a Grandmother?" History, Pseudo-History and Genre in **Doctor Who**' in Butler, David, ed, *Time and Relative Dissertations in Space: Critical Perspectives on Doctor Who*, p63.

[42] Mathieson, Jamie, in Arnopp, Jason, 'Episode Preview: *The Girl Who Died*', *Doctor Who Magazine* (DWM) #492.

originally have beaten pedants at their own game by explaining how these particular Vikings based their horned helmets on those worn by the Mire while in the village on previous visits[43].

In other respects, as we have seen, the 'theme-park history' version of the Vikings – those fearsome fighters of legend – is entirely undermined. Instead of adhering to conventional depictions, *The Girl Who Died* subverts them by quickly dispensing with the idea of hyper-masculine warrior Vikings and focussing instead on farmers and fishermen who are utterly unaccustomed to warfare. Another way of looking at this is not so much as playing with history at all, but as playing with genre: in this case, poking fun at the genre of self-serious, dour, and gritty 'Viking stories' discussed above. A huge amount of **Doctor Who** can be best understood as dropping the regular cast into less of a fully realised world so much as a pre-existing category of story[44], which the show

---

[43] TCH #81, p90. Seyfried, Stewart, '**Doctor Who** – Series 9 Deleted Scene – *The Girl Who Died*' makes it clear that the Mire have made several previous visits, and also briefly shows a Viking scroll on which the Mire are depicted wearing horned helmets. These scrolls are also a mix of accurate and inaccurate – the runes used date from the 12th century rather than Younger Futhark as they should be, three hundred years out of time; but the runes' particular units of meaning such as 'cattle', 'man', 'harvest', 'journey', and 'Óðinn' do suggest that thought had gone into 'a list of approved words' (Chris Lees, concept designer for this story, personal communication with author). The scrolls can be examined in more detail at the BBC **Doctor Who** Instagram posts listed in the bibliography.

[44] Sandifer, Elizabeth, *TARDIS Eruditorum: An Unofficial Critical History of Doctor Who Volume 4: Tom Baker and the Hinchcliffe Years*, pp109-10.

can then play straight or distort as it sees fit, and the programme has regularly played with subverting genre standards or typical story templates over the years. Indeed, in fiction at least, there is very little separating the two: 'history is a construct of the present. Viewed through the prism of popular fiction it can become genre'[45].

One of the more recent manifestations of that playfulness is the 'celebrity mythological'. A riff on fan nomenclature for **Who** story types such as 'pseudo-historical' and 'celebrity historical', the term describes a subgenre, specific to the Capaldi era, in which the Doctor encounters famous folk heroes or gods instead of 'real' historical figures. Examples include Robin Hood, Santa Claus, a 'store-brand Superman', and even (a version of) Óðinn. Highlighting *The Girl Who Died*, Max Kashevsky observes that masculinity – and whether to embrace or reject particular narratives around masculinity – is one of the cornerstones of this subgenre; note that the examples are all 'mythical men'[46]. Placing the Doctor alongside other fictional characters from folklore and mythology sparks discussions about what male heroes should look like in the stories that we tell.

Inevitably, the other hallmark of a subgenre clashing together fictional characters from different stories is metafiction. Here it is

---

[45] O'Mahony, '"Now How is That Wolf Able to Impersonate a Grandmother?"', p62.

[46] Kashevsky, Max, 'Folk Heroes and the Doctor: **Doctor Who**'s "Mythological Celebrity" Stories'. Kashevsky's other examples can be found in *Robot of Sherwood* (2014), *Last Christmas* (2014), and *The Return of Doctor Mysterio* (2016).

worth dwelling for a moment on how *The Girl Who Died*'s playing fast-and-loose with historical accuracy is potentially rather in keeping with Old Norse-Icelandic literature – especially in examples that appear to play history for laughs and entertainment. In *Ynglinga Saga*, the first saga contained within his history of the kings of Norway, the 14th-century Icelandic historian Snorri Sturluson (along with the poet Þjóðólfr ór Hvini, the verses of whose poem *Ynglingatal* Snorri cites as historical evidence) is perfectly happy to undermine certain kings by recounting their implausibly ludicrous demises: drowning in a vat of mead when going out at night to urinate[47], drunkenly accepting the invitation of a magical dwarf to 'meet Odin' (a stock euphemism for 'die')[48], or being slain by a pitchfork thrown by a 'slave workman', shortly after waging a war for the sake of a much-loved pet sparrow[49]. To what extent this litany of embarrassing and unceremonious deaths – for many such kings the only detail recorded about them – is remotely accurate, or deliberately embellished as part of 'sagnaskemmtan' (saga-entertainment), we do not know.

Multiple sagas even include self-conscious and playful statements that could indicate such narratives were to be thought of as at least partially fictional. In *Göngu-Hrólfs Saga*, the audience is told 'even if people think such a thing incredible, it's still everyone's responsibility to say whatever he's seen or heard. And it isn't easy

---

[47] Snorri Sturluson, in Finlay, Alison and Anthony Faulkes, trans, *Heimskringla – Volume 1: The Beginnings to Óláfr Tryggvason*, p15.
[48] Snorri Sturluson, *Heimskringla Vol 1*, p16; see also Goeres, Erin Michelle, *The Poetics of Commemoration: Skaldic Verse and Social Memory, c890-1070*, p35.
[49] Snorri Sturluson, *Heimskringla Vol 1*, pp20-21.

to contradict what has been said in the past by men of learning'[50]. Snorri Sturluson says in the prologue to his Norwegian history that 'although we do not know how true [the stories recounted in oral poetry] are, we know of cases where learned men of old have **taken** such things to be true'[51]. Whether such comments indicate that saga-material was intended to be received as fictitious, whether it was to be received as 'true history' by most but with knowing nods towards fictionality for those in the know, or whether they represent careful, respectful self-distancing of Christian writers and audiences from the claims of pagan mythology (as seems plausible in Snorri's case), is hotly debated[52].

The notion that, in terms of Norse-Icelandic retellings, 'no conceptual distinction was made between history and story,' and that '**saga** referred to anything that was 'said' as history; as such it contained its own claim to truth,'[53] strongly resembles various thematic assertions that Moffat puts in the mouths of his characters during his years on **Doctor Who**. The most famous two are undoubtedly 'We're all stories in the end' and 'Every story ever told really happened. Stories are where memories go when they're forgotten,' although there are also multiple instances of characters finding themselves trapped within the parameters of a story, as well as Robin Hood recognising the Doctor as another fictional

---

[50] Pálsson and Edwards, *Göngu-Hrolf's Saga*, p84.
[51] Snorri Sturluson, *Heimskringla Vol 1*, p3 (emphasis mine).
[52] See, e.g., O'Connor, Ralph, 'History or Fiction? Truth-Claims and Defensive Narrators in Icelandic Romance-Sagas', in *Mediaeval Scandinavia* 15, pp101-69.
[53] Hastrup, 'Uchronia and the Two Histories of Iceland, 1400-1800' in Hastrup, ed, *Other Histories*, p112 (emphasis in original).

construct when he tells him 'I'm just as real as you are'[54]. Cut dialogue from the story would have recognised this implicitly – Ashildr was said to be 'working on the saga of tomorrow's battle', while another character 'felt [the Doctor] would make a fine saga'[55].

This phenomenon – of Viking history as story: as folk memory and saga – resulted in what Kirsten Hastrup has labelled 'uchronia', itself a very **Doctor Who**ish concept; as she defines it, uchronia is 'nowhere in time [...] a separate history, a history, so to speak, out of time'[56]. It refers to a collective memory of the past which may not be terribly accurate, but whose accuracy matters less than its lingering power over the present. In one sense, uchronia is another version of 'theme-park history' – how we choose to remember events a certain way – and one with which **Doctor Who**, as a product of the postcolonial, postmodern Britain of the late 20th and early 21st centuries, is intimately connected. There is a case that it is the ultimate postmodern programme because of its 'ideology of anachronism'[57]. In other words, it can quite happily throw the ordered linearity of history under a bus and introduce 'atomic bazookas and police boxes into 11th-century England'[58]. A

---

[54] *The Big Bang* (2010); *Hell Bent* (2015); various examples including *The Pandorica Opens* (2010), *Sleep No More* (2015), and *Extremis* (2017); *Robot of Sherwood*.
[55] TCH #81, pp118, 96.
[56] Hastrup, 'Uchronia and the Two Histories of Iceland', p113. Comparable to 'utopia' or 'no place'.
[57] Charles, Alec, 'The Ideology of Anachronism: Television, History and the Nature of Time', in Butler, ed, *Time and Relative Dissertations in Space*, p121.
[58] Charles, 'The Ideology of Anachronism', p112, in reference to *The*

few episodes before *The Girl Who Died*, indeed, the Doctor glories in the chaos of his own 'anachronisms', a word which is explicitly applied to his ostentatiously parading around sunglasses, an electric guitar, and an army tank in 12th-century Essex[59].

Doctor Who on television is uniquely well-suited to juxtaposing the strange and the mundane, images and visuals that do not belong together, making weird collages that are perfect for our rapidly channel-hopping 'era of historical mélange'[60]. Going one step further, it can mix and match genres, stories, and myths that do not seem to belong together – such as blending **Dad's Army**, **Monty Python's Flying Circus**, and the trappings of Norse mythology. To highlight historical inaccuracy and continuity errors in a show that wilfully embraces its ideology of anachronism is to almost miss the point. The openly artificial uchronia in which this programme operates draws on the strength of its own playful fictionality – and of its encounters with other myths, ancient and modern – to poke holes in that which is commonly supposed to be 'realistic'. Just as the narrative of the Mire as an all-powerful, marauding army is undermined by a bit of fakery and sleight-of-hand with a wooden puppet, so too is the popular narrative of hyper-masculine Viking history subverted by a few horned helmets, some electric eels, and bizarre sights accessed by a box that's bigger on the inside. How else should we describe television, after all?

Time Meddler (1965).

[59] *The Magician's Apprentice* (2015).

[60] Charles, 'The Ideology of Anachronism', p112.

CHAPTER 2: NOBODY EXPECTS... EELS! THE IMPORTANCE OF BEING SILLY

The first chapter identified the fact that *The Girl Who Died* is, at least partially, about mocking the ridiculous excesses associated with toxic masculinity. But the story should not only be defined in terms of what it argues **against**, but also what it argues **for**. It has clearly aimed a degree of satire and parody at self-serious warmongering and unhealthy ideas about what constitutes manliness. But is there anything put forward in its place? This chapter identifies *The Girl Who Died* as making a positive argument for what can only be described as silliness. The important social function laughter can play – in both modern and medieval contexts – will be highlighted, but also thrown into sharp relief by discussing the alarmingly dangerous target of the story's satire. Mocking toxic masculinity in general is one thing, but in an explicitly Norse context, the masculinism of far-right and white supremacist movements loom particularly large... and such spectres are far from a laughing matter.

2.1: 'Babies Think that Laughter is Singing'

In addition to Norse mythology and certain Western and samurai films[61], *The Girl Who Died* owes a clear debt to British television

---

[61] *High Noon* (1952), *Seven Samurai* (1954), and *The Magnificent Seven* (1960), especially the trope of a village under threat from outside forces and being protected by a small group of heroes making a desperate last stand (TCH #81, p87; Arnopp, 'Episode Preview'). The latter two films also champion the bravery of farmers over rapacious warriors and bandits. Director Ed Bazalgette watched *Seven Samurai* 'to set a visual style for the

comedy classics of the late 20th century. The two most prominent influences in that regard are the aforementioned **Monty Python's Flying Circus** and **Dad's Army**, both of which aired during the original run of **Doctor Who** and have subsequently entered television legend (the former has even spawned its own adjective – 'Pythonesque'). A reference to a third comedy classic, **The Benny Hill Show** (1955-89), comes in the form of 'the Benny Hill theme', an infamously goofy piece of music also known as 'Yakety Sax'[62] – not actually the show's theme music, but played sufficiently regularly that it became inextricably associated with it. The piece is here overlaid over footage of the Mire's ignominious defeat, in what Mathieson has called 'my favourite joke I've ever written in anything'[63].

The **Dad's Army** similarities predominantly revolve around the bunch of rag-tag, unskilled Vikings placed into a warfare situation, echoing the Home Guard in the original sitcom. The notion of 'rubbish Vikings' was Moffat's favourite element of Mathieson's proposed storyline, which he encouraged him to run with; the main premise of the earlier programme was taken as a direct inspiration for this aspect of the story[64]. At one point in the script, the character of Einarr, trying to put himself forward as the new village chieftain, was described as having 'shades of Captain

---

episode' (TCH #81, p98) as well as a more conventional choice, *The Vikings* (1958).

[62] Written by James Q 'Spider' Rich and Boots Randolph, and recorded by the latter in 1963.

[63] Arnopp, 'Episode Preview'.

[64] TCH #81, p87; Arnopp, 'Episode Preview'.

Mainwaring'[65], referring to the leader of the Walmington-on-Sea platoon in the sitcom. During filming, dialogue was added making the comparison even more explicit, with Clara telling the Doctor 'You've got the Vikings' answer to **Dad's Army**'[66]; the scene was filmed but eventually cut, although it is preserved on the DVD boxset and can be viewed on YouTube[67]. In the episode as broadcast, there are no longer any direct references, but the influence is nonetheless clear.

The Girl Who Died thus removes the archetype of 'hapless dupes who have a serious task to perform' from the context of the Second World War and places them in a Viking milieu instead. A by-product of this is the shedding of any sense of patriotic pride audiences can be encouraged to take in the fundamental, well-meaning decency of the British armed forces. Instead, these qualities are transposed to the Vikings – a fascinating decision, given that they were historically (albeit much more distantly) invaders of Britain, much as the Nazis threatened to be. British programmes featuring the Vikings – such as **The Last Kingdom** – largely (and understandably) identify with the English, depicting the Norsemen as an existential threat to their way of life, even while appreciating or admiring certain aspects of Viking culture. In yet another example of the story overturning as many stock tropes as possible and challenging common assumptions, a British audience is invited here to consider that their hostile invaders of the past are comparable to their much-loved wartime heroes.

---

[65] TCH #81, p96.

[66] TCH #81, pp105, 118.

[67] Seyfried, '**Doctor Who** – Series 9 Deleted Scene'.

The other major comic influence on the episode is the surrealist humour of the Monty Python comedy troupe. One episode of their television programme, **Monty Python's Flying Circus**, features the 'Spam' sketch, in which a group of Vikings appear in a 20th-century greasy spoon café, going on to sing a 'Spam Song' which is itself a riff on Samuel Coleridge-Taylor's non-humorous 'Viking Song' (1911). As with **Norsemen** and *The Girl Who Died*, the Viking figures are not inherently funny in themselves but become so when juxtaposed with a modern setting or modern sensibilities. This is a recurring Monty Python trick: embracing the illogical, the implausible, and the downright nonsensical. Such an anarchic sense of humour is a good fit for a science-fantasy programme that also revels in bizarre and incongruous juxtapositions. These sorts of juxtapositions are arguably core to what **Doctor Who** does, right back to its very first cliffhanger of a 1960s police box appearing in a Stone Age wasteland.

More influential than the television programme, however, is the film *Monty Python and the Holy Grail* (1975). It was directed by Terry Jones, the medievalist of the group; he also wrote books and presented documentaries on medieval history and directed the aforementioned *Erik the Viking*. Nominally set less than a century after *The Girl Who Died*, *Holy Grail* boasts a plethora of stock medieval tropes, from Arthurian romance to the persecution of witches (no Vikings appear, although a vessel similar in design to a Viking longboat does). At first glance, it looks as though the film is embracing a modern phenomenon wherein 'the Middle Ages [have] become an object of laughter'[68]. David Matthews suggests,

---

[68] D'Arcens, Louise, 'Medievalist Laughter', in *postmedieval* 5:2

however, that the film is knowingly poking fun at modern depictions of the medieval period rather than laughing at the medieval period itself: the stereotypes are too extreme, the depiction too obviously inaccurate and anachronistic, and the humour too incongruous[69]. This manifests in multiple jokes about the artifice involved in the modern-day attempting to depict the medieval: knights pretend to be on horseback but are actually just followed around by squires knocking two coconuts together, the castle of Camelot is dismissed as 'only a model', and 20th-century political ideals are put into the mouths of medieval peasantry.

The Girl Who Died is not quite as self-aware or surreal in comparison, although it does borrow some key iconography: the floating head of 'Odin' appearing in the sky is a direct visual reference to the floating head of God in the Python film[70]. The implausible and deeply silly use of animals – electric eels to create a current of electricity in the ninth century, in this case – also

---

'Comic Medievalism', p116.

[69] Matthews, David, 'Said in Jest: Who's Laughing at the Middle Ages (and When)?', in *postmedieval* 5:2 'Comic Medievalism', p127. Matthews traces this phenomenon of using medieval tropes to comedic excess as a way of commenting on the folly of the present as far back as Miguel de Cervantes' *Don Quixote* (1612), pp128-30.

[70] As noted by various reviewers and critics (Cooper, Steven, *Steven Moffat's Doctor Who 2014-2015: The Critical Fan's Guide to Peter Capaldi's Doctor (Unauthorized)*, p153; Burk, Graeme and Robert Smith?, *Who Is the Doctor 2: The Unofficial Guide to Doctor Who – the Modern Series*, p179; Graham, 'A Surfeit of Lampreys'); other elements of the drafts were also 'positively **Monty Python**-esque' (Arnopp, Jason, 'Immortal Words: The 2015 Team! Jamie Mathieson', DWM #493).

resembles the use to which animals are put in *Holy Grail* (from livestock catapulted over the castle ramparts to a murderous bunny rabbit), or indeed the comic screaming goats in *Thor: Love and Thunder*.

It is this sense of incongruous humour which was particularly criticised by reviewers and critics – especially when juxtaposed with the episode's more serious segments as it tries to tell a moving tale about, well, a girl who died. One such reviewer declares that 'perhaps the issue is that the episode's tone is wildly uneven... [it] incorporates so many disparate tone shifts as to suffer from identity crisis', another that the episode 'really suffers from the complete failure to decide whether or not it's meant to be funny'[71]. The story's reliance on knockabout comedy runs throughout the Doctor's efforts to train up the village of Vikings, reaching a peak in their final confrontation with the Mire. From the disembodied head of 'Odin' to sight gags regarding the villagers' incompetence with weapons training, from an explicitly 'rubbish' wooden puppet scaring off a crack squad of alien invaders to that same footage being set to 'the Benny Hill theme', there is an explicit vein here of what can only be called silliness. This is the sort of thing one might expect in a pantomime, surely, not a programme being subjected to 'serious' critical analysis.

Yet there is significant method in the madness; the silliness is systematic. To discuss it, we must turn to the Russian literary critic Mikhail Bakhtin's theory of laughter and the carnivalesque as having a healthy and cathartic social function. In *Problems of*

---

[71] Hassell, Clint, '*The Girl Who Died* Review'; Elledge, Jonn, Tweet posted 21 March 2022.

Dostoevsky's Poetics (1963) and *Rabelais and His World* (1965), Bakhtin outlined the literary mode of the carnivalesque, particularly in reference to medieval societies, but also in the more modern example of Fyodor Dostoevsky's 19th-century novels.

As Bakhtin describes it, carnival functioned in the medieval sphere by using anarchic humour to provide (temporary) liberation from a 'given social order'[72]. Readers may be familiar with the Roman festival of Saturnalia, or the tradition of a Lord of Misrule presiding over a Feast of Fools, both of which involved overturning conventional social norms and hierarchies. Satire or mockery of those in power was permitted for a given period, as was the unregulated fusing together of seriousness and silliness. Bakhtin writes that, in carnival:

> 'what is suspended first of all is hierarchical structure and all the forms of terror, reverence, piety, and etiquette connected with it [...] carnival brings together, unifies, weds, and combines the sacred with the profane, the lofty with the low, the great with the insignificant, the wise with the stupid.'[73]

The comparisons to *The Girl Who Died* and the way in which it shifts from comic to tragic, ridiculous to sublime, are clear. Apparently jarring tonal shifts from deeply serious to frivolous subject matter are not just present in this story; they are a fundamental feature of human imagination and creativity, right back to the Greeks' satyr plays, which presented a parodic contrast

---

[72] Bakhtin, Mikhail, *Problems of Dostoevsky's Poetics*, p160.
[73] Bakhtin, *Problems of Dostoevsky's Poetics*, p123.

with the tragedy audiences had been watching moments before. Additionally, our 'hierarchical structure' – a rigid hegemony of hyper-masculinity – is gleefully dismantled, as heroes who are conventionally unimpressive, or feminine, or queer, thwart the bullies of the cosmos.

Other features of the carnivalesque include:

a. 'everyone [being] an active participant'.

b. the fact that 'the heroes of myth and the historical figures of the past are deliberately and emphatically contemporised'.

c. 'an extraordinary freedom of plot and philosophical invention... bold and unrestrained use of the fantastic and adventure'.

d. 'concern with current and topical issues'.

e. 'the discovery of the inner man – "one's own self", accessible not to passive self-observation but only through an active dialogic approach to one's own self'.

f. the phenomenon of 'eccentricity, the violation of the usual and the generally accepted'.

Lastly, Bakhtin observes that the spirit of the medieval carnivalesque has survived by being 'reincarnated in literature'[74] – and now in television.

Appropriately, these features can all be detected in *The Girl Who Died*. With regard to **a.**, the entire village community is brought together in a party atmosphere towards the story's end, dancing and feasting and drinking as the supposed deadliest warriors in the

---

[74] Bakhtin, *Problems of Dostoevsky's Poetics*, pp122, 108, 113, 118, 120, 126, 157.

galaxy approach. Mathieson and Moffat are careful to give a role to as many of the Vikings as possible: Einarr (or 'Chuckles') powers up the electric current; 'ZZ Top' films proceedings on Clara's mobile phone; Brot (or 'Lofty') has the task of tossing quoit-like coils of wire onto the aerials projected out of the Mire's armour, disguised as a game that is part of the general merriment; and it is Ashildr who projects the image of the fearsome monster which scares the Mire off. There is something fundamentally democratic and egalitarian about the carnivalesque mode: everyone pitches in.

The presence of blatant anachronisms and the interaction of the distant past with recognisable aspects of the 21st-century viewer's world illustrate **b.** A supposed deity – Odin – seems to turn up, only to be rendered much less mythic than he should be. Similarly, the Vikings themselves are 'contemporised' by being viewed through a much less reverent lens that does not regard them as hyper-masculine warriors, but either as figures of fun or as fundamentally ordinary and relatable people: some scared, some rather silly, others motivated by love of family. The episode also avoids putting overly cod-medieval dialogue in the mouths of its Viking characters and even on occasion opts for modern cadences: 'I think he was being sarcastic', 'I'm not good with heights', and 'They **what**?'.

In terms of **c.**, this story is not merely fantastical – Vikings are attacked by military lampreys from space – but the means by which the Doctor and company fight back against their enemies revolves around ingenuity, showcasing 'extraordinary freedom' and 'invention'. This is something most **Doctor Who** stories aim for – consider the dictum that the programme is fundamentally about 'the triumph of intellect and romance over brute force and cynicism'[75] – but is even more the case here. The Doctor and Clara are stranded in ninth-century Scandinavia, without the TARDIS or a trusty sonic gadget, stripped of their usual handy plot resolution tools. Much like characters in **MacGyver** (1985-92, 2016-21) or **The A-Team** (1983-87)[76], they must make inventive use of low-tech materials around them to solve the problem of the day, and eventually do so through the use of unexpected (and historically improbable) electric eels, ropey special effects, and a teenage girl's imagination, all prompted by the translated cries of a baby.

We will return to **d.** in the third section of this chapter, which looks at how the story does indeed echo a very current, topical issue, namely the far right's obsession with Norse mythology. Meanwhile, **e.** identifies the more introspective elements of carnival – that in challenging social norms it allows participants to look inwards and discover something fundamental about themselves and their identity. This occurs in the form of the Doctor's recognition of where he has seen his own face before and why he subconsciously picked it, and what this says about who he is as a person. We even get Bakhtin's 'dialogic approach to one's own self' in the form of the flashback of the 10th Doctor directly influencing the actions of the 12th. This will be treated in greater depth in the following chapter.

Finally, Bakhtin refers in **f.** to 'eccentricity', a word commonly applied to the Doctor, even sometimes within the programme

---

[75] Ferguson, Craig, 'The Lost **Doctor Who** Cold Open'.
[76] Both of which Mathieson has cited as influencing this episode (TCH #81, p87; Arnopp, 'Episode Preview').

itself[77], but also to 'the violation of the usual and the generally accepted'. As pointed out in the introduction, subverting received wisdom about various matters – the Vikings, history itself, gender roles, our own perceptions – is a key part of what *The Girl Who Died* is doing. One additional subversion is its idea that laughter and silliness are valuable and profound, rather than something childish to look down on. This again echoes Bakhtin, who writes that the power of laughter is such that:

> 'the world is seen anew, no less (and perhaps more) profoundly than when seen from the serious standpoint. Therefore, laughter is just as admissible in great literature, posing universal problems, as seriousness. Certain essential aspects of the world are accessible only to laughter'.[78]

Indeed, laughter is recontextualised as something babies understand as 'singing': an involuntary response of delight or amusement becomes instead a deliberate, heartfelt, creative expression of pure joy. No longer childish, but childlike. In short, we have arrived at what the episode stands for – an ethics of laughter.

2.2: 'Look Happy! Winning is All About Looking Happier than the Other Guy!'

Appropriately, Bakhtin's theory of the carnivalesque and the power of laughter has its roots in the medieval world. He writes, 'medieval

---

[77] E.g., *The Silurians* (1970) episode 4; *Colony in Space* (1971) episode 2; *The Time Warrior* (1973-74) episode 2; *The Mark of the Rani* (1985) episode 1.

[78] Bakhtin, Mikhail, *Rabelais and His World*, p66.

and Renaissance folk culture was familiar with the element of terror only as represented by comic monsters, who were defeated by laughter', a defeat which represented the 'victory of laughter over fear'[79]. In this schema, fear meant 'the extreme expression of narrow-minded and stupid seriousness'[80] – that which terrified ordinary people and kept them in their place: officialdom, asceticism, and adherence to rigid dogma or ideology. In the medieval imagination, laughter at the events of a performed work functioned as an apotropaic force – something capable of holding certain evils at bay[81].

This is exactly how it works in *The Girl Who Died*, where the evil being held at bay is toxic masculinity. One of the most insightful assertions anyone has made about the story is Jack Graham's claim that it is explicitly about 'the importance of being silly'. The allegedly serious ideals of militarism and nobility in battle are roundly mocked in the form of both the Viking and the Mire warriors, their folly laid bare in various ways… but what is crucial is that they do not recognise this folly in themselves. The Mire are irredeemably self-serious, despite being blatantly ludicrous warrior lampreys from space in a family show made by the BBC. They are ultimately thwarted because of a deeply insecure fear of being laughed at, panicking over a comic video of them going intergalactically viral. More than anything, they want to avoid looking silly – and the harder they try, the dafter they look.

---

[79] Bakhtin, *Rabelais and His World*, pp39, 90.

[80] Bakhtin, *Rabelais and His World*, p47.

[81] Quast, Bruno, *Vom Kult zur Kunst. Öffnungen des rituellen Textes in Mittelalter und Früher Neuzeit*, pp124-25.

Contrast this with our heroic characters: the Doctor, Ashildr, the shoddy warriors. As Graham identifies, they are all variously presented as 'silly' in one way or another. The Doctor goofs around with a feeble yo-yo routine; jokes left, right, and centre; and comes up with absurd (and blatantly anachronistic) nicknames for his not-so-crack team of warriors. Ashildr could be called silly for retreating to her own hut and sword-fighting against a wooden mock-up of 'Odin'; it is her own foolish declaration of war on the Mire that seems set to spell doom on the village; and her wooden puppet of a creature 'from a nightmare' is explicitly not very good. The villagers are similarly painted in a ridiculous light, choosing to stay and fight against an enemy they cannot possibly hope to defeat: 'we might admire the courage', as Graham says, 'but it's still silly when looked at in purely pragmatic terms.'[82] When the Mire arrive to do battle, the heroes are dancing and pratfalling and generally making merry – self-evidently a nonsensical thing to do in the face of a ruthless army.

Even the electric eels are deeply, anachronistically silly, in a way that is very in keeping with Monty Python's brand of incongruous humour. It has been described as something of a 'plot hole' that electric eels – creatures native to South America – appear in a Scandinavian village, with naturalist Chris Packham labelling the choice 'a shocking error!'[83] One could plausibly mount a defence by citing the Vikings' extensive trading networks that led to cornelian beads from Gujarat being found as far afield as Derbyshire[84]; the

---

[82] Graham, 'A Surfeit of Lampreys'.

[83] Cited in Holmes, Jonathan, 'Was This a Shocking Plot Hole in **Doctor Who:** *The Girl Who Died*?', *RadioTimes*.

[84] Jarman, *River Kings* (passim, but especially pp1-7 and 291-99).

1928 film *The Viking* sets a precedent by including an exotic parrot among the Norwegians, either received through trade or claimed as a spoil of war. But, as in the previous chapter, to criticise or defend the programme for this in terms of historical accuracy is to miss that the eels are a deliberate, knowing anachronism – just look at the giddy delight on the Doctor's face when he finds them where he least expects. They fit neatly into Moffat's recurring trope of fish as inherently, incongruously comic[85], which may well stem from the 'Find the Fish' segment in *Monty Python's The Meaning of Life* (1983) or could perhaps have been influenced by the *Eels* episode of the surreal comedy show **The Mighty Boosh** (2004-07). Both regular eels and electric eels (which are not actually eels at all) are especially unusual creatures that have long flummoxed scientists[86], making them oddly fitting for a pointed

---

[85] Among other examples: 'fish fingers and custard' is an early indicator of the eccentricity of the 11th Doctor; he also offers the excuse of checking for 'an escaped fish' while examining a glass of water in *The Beast Below* (2010); fish implausibly swimming through fog are central to *A Christmas Carol* (2010); he and River Song refer on multiple occasions to their mutual friend 'Jim the Fish'; and the minisode 'Bad Night' (2011) has a farcical plot revolving around the Queen having been turned into a goldfish.

[86] As Patrik Svensson puts it, 'science has come up against many mysteries, but few have proven as intractable and difficult to solve as the eel' (*The Gospel of the Eels: A Father, a Son and the World's Most Enigmatic Fish*, p20). This is a creature effectively capable of 'suspending its own aging', waiting for decades for the right moment to achieve sexual maturity (p150); Aristotle thought it an utterly implausible miracle of being (pp15-19); and it baffled and frustrated the young Sigmund Freud (pp37-51). The electric eel, meanwhile, was in 2015 thought completely unique and 'monotypic', the only species within its genus; it can deliver electric

swerve into an explicitly silly plot resolution. To coin a phrase, reality can be sillier than fiction.

Crucially, it is **because** of their silliness that these characters (including the eels!) are able to defeat opponents who take themselves extremely seriously. Bakhtin's carnivalesque laughter might be 'mocking, deriding' but it is also 'gay, triumphant, and at the same time […] **directed at those who laugh**'[87]. In other words, an ethics of laughter involves not just laughing at the ridiculousness of others, but at the ridiculousness of oneself. 'That is rubbish,' Clara says of Ashildr's wooden puppet; 'I know,' the Doctor responds gleefully, proud of just quite how poor an effort it is. He outright encourages the villagers to 'Look happy!' because, as he puts it, 'Winning is all about looking happier than the other guy'. Humour is frequently about the difference between how things seem to be and how things actually are – a gulf in which *The Girl Who Died* is particularly interested – meaning those who 'get the joke' are essentially seeing the world more clearly. Accepting one's own silliness grants you power over it and facilitates Bakhtin's 'victory of laughter over fear'.

It is significant that the Doctor is in on the joke here, in contrast to the way his utter seriousness made him the unwitting butt of the joke in the previous season's medievalist tale *Robot of Sherwood*[88].

---

shocks of up to 860 volts but can also use this capability as a form of radar or to paralyse prey before reaching it; and 80% of its body is made up of electric organs (Heimbuch, Jaymi, '8 Shocking Facts About Electric Eels').

[87] Bakhtin, *Rabelais and His World*, p11-12 (emphasis mine).

[88] The two stories make for an intriguing pairing, and at one point Mathieson conceived of the story as 'the *Robot of Sherwood* slot, in

There, 'the Doctor takes his own role as an objective observer very seriously [...] and laughter threatens to undermine his belief in his own role', to the point that he even 'represents a sort of intolerance of laughter'[89] (most notably Robin's). Throughout the story, the Doctor engages in an entertainingly puerile competition with his equally fictional opposite number, Robin Hood, both about who is more objectively 'real' but also who deserves the hero role in the narrative. The two leading men big themselves up by trying to put the other down, much like combatants in the Norse mannjafnaðir tradition. By the time of *The Girl Who Died*, this particular Doctor has grown wiser – that is to say, less self-serious, and more open to silliness. He is now quite comfortable adopting apotropaic laughter to keep this particular brand of self-serious toxic masculinity at bay, and he starts by shedding his own. By the time of his final words before he regenerates into the 13th Doctor, it has even become a key part of his credo: 'Laugh hard, run fast, be kind'[90]. As will be discussed at greater length, the character is in the

---

terms of a gag-heavy historical episode', whilst also noting that it has something of a darker undercurrent (in Arnopp, 'Episode Preview').

[89] Vishnuvajjala, Usha, 'Objectivity, Impossibility and Laughter in **Doctor Who**'s *Robot of Sherwood*', in Fugelso, Karl, ed, *Politics and Medievalism*, pp212, 214. It is also notable that, in the deleted scene already mentioned, the Doctor recognises that Clara's boyfriend from the previous season, Danny Pink, 'would laugh his head off' at the absurdity of the Doctor training an amateurish Viking army, and seems to approve of the idea, suggesting he is much more open to being laughed at these days.

[90] *Twice Upon a Time* (2017). For more on the progressive rejection of masculinity during the Capaldi era, see particularly Franke, Alyssa, *The Black Archive #22: Hell Bent*, and Mooney, Darren, *The*

wider sense a prime example of a clown-trickster figure: someone who is 'not confined by boundaries, conceptual, social, or physical, and can cross lines that are impermeable to normal individuals'[91]. Once again, narrative power is conferred on characters who can weaponise humour[92].

Why is this important? Why bother with theories of laughter at all? Is this not the ultimate example of killing a joke by explaining it? But it matters because what we laugh at says a lot about who we are, about our societal norms and values. Whether jokes are targeted at the more or the less powerful. Whether we are punching up or punching down. One critic writes that 'what the social entity laughs at, and most of what it laughs against [...] indicates what is not acceptable to it.'[93] What we are mocking when we laugh is especially vital to consider in an age where comedians like Ricky Gervais and Dave Chappelle can make a living out of demonising trans people and then telling audiences not to be offended by vicious attacks on a marginalised minority disguised as 'jokes'[94].

Furthermore, humour is good for us – it is well-known that, 'in response to laughter, our bodies produce pain relieving endorphins, returning the body to a more relaxed state', and

---

Black Archive #59: Kill the Moon.

[91] Stott, Andrew, *Comedy: The New Critical Idiom*, p51.

[92] This makes a pleasing parallel with the power of laughter utilised by Sam Swift's comic routine in the very next episode, *The Woman Who Lived*.

[93] Hertzler, Joyce O, *Laughter: A Socio-Scientific Analysis*, p94.

[94] Lawler, Kelly, 'From Ricky Gervais to Dave Chappelle, Netflix has a Trans-Bashing Comedy Problem'.

scientific studies have also backed up the idea that playful thinking, even in adults, can yield better solutions to problems[95]. Cliché though it might be, it is not far off the mark to say that in some situations, laughter really **is** the best medicine. This is even more the case in the phenomenon of laughing at oneself, to engage in what Bakhtin calls 'ridicule [...] fused with rejoicing'[96]: this, too, is fundamentally apotropaic, keeping the demons of self-seriousness at bay. Both in terms of personal health and in a wider sense of the health of society, laughter is – or at its best, can be – a profound and powerful force for good.

That is certainly the belief of radical activist clowns, who implement the power of humour in reality rather than just in theory, and who follow the mantra that 'mocking and utterly confusing the enemy can be more powerful than direct confrontation.'[97] It is also the logic followed by satirists and parodists, many of whom clearly get under the skin of the politicians and powerful individuals they ridicule. Readers may recall various instances of satirical depictions of world leaders being met with aggressive responses[98]. The archetypal 'strongman' leader fears humour because it diminishes him, makes him look

---

[95] Bala, Michael, 'The Clown: An Archetypal Self-Journey', *Jung Journal: Culture and Psyche* 4:1, p55; Proyer, René T, 'A new Structural Model for the Study of Adult Playfulness: Assessment and Exploration of an Understudied Individual Differences Variable', *Personality and Individual Differences* 108, pp113-22.

[96] Bakhtin, *Problems of Dostoevsky's Poetics*, p126.

[97] Beautiful Trouble, 'Clandestine Insurgent Rebel Clown Army'.

[98] 'Jacob Zuma Painting: ANC to Sue South Africa's Brett Murray'; 'Erdogan Poem: Turkey Demands German Action over "Obscene" Satirist'; 'Kremlin Pulls Strings on TV Puppets' (all BBC News).

weak. Which raises the question – how effective is this apotropaic laughter in the real world?

2.3: 'War is Our Way'

In a pivot worthy of the episode itself, focus must now turn towards something very serious indeed. The subversions discussed in these first two chapters are distinctly politically barbed and have a direct target in the form of horrifying real-world movements. To mock toxic, warfare-obsessed masculinity dressed up in Viking imagery in the 2010s is, intentionally or not, to make fun of the far right and neo-Nazism.

The connection between Norse mythology and Scandinavian ancestry on the one hand, and virulent white supremacism and Nazism on the other, dates back to the 19th century. There is insufficient space here to fully unpack the complex lattice of interweaving influences which led to these associations. Suffice to say that among them include centuries of European antisemitism (especially in the hugely significant work of Martin Luther, whose impact on German language and, by extension, culture cannot be overstated), the 'Germanic Romanticism' of the Grimm Brothers, the late-19th-century völkisch or people's movement aiming to cultivate a German nation-state, and the reworking of Norse mythological motifs by opera composer (and noted antisemite) Richard Wagner[99]. Quests to unearth and revive a mythic past as a basis for modern national and ethnic identity are fundamentally

---

[99] Árni Björnsson, *Wagner and the Volsungs: Icelandic Sources of* Der Ring des Nibelungen, pp25, 41-3, 69-80.

'dependent on operations of exclusion'[100], separating approved in-groups from spurned out-groups. Among the modern far right, this latter category chiefly consists of Muslims, Jews, and people of colour.

Hateful racialised presentations of the medieval world have similarly poisoned the scholarly field of Norse studies for decades. Examples include Gustav Neckel, who 'blam[ed] socialism, Jews, and class revolutions for the "decline" of a Germanic race [he] saw descending from this Viking past'[101], and philologist Jan de Vries, who collaborated with the Nazis during the Second World War[102]. Scholars' findings influenced Nazi policy in various ways, and vice-versa. The idea of 'Männerbünde' ('all-male warrior associations in so-called primitive societies'), which had been floated by ethnologists, theorists, and folklorists, inspired aspects of the SS and its predecessor the SA, and in return Himmler's Ahnenerbe thinktank funded excavations of Viking sites[103]. Elsewhere, Viking Age burial mounds formed the backdrop to speeches by the

---

[100] von Schnurbein, Stefanie, *Norse Revival: Transformations of German Neopaganism*, p26.

[101] Kim, Dorothy, 'White Supremacists Have Weaponized an Imaginary Viking Past. It's Time to Reclaim the Real History'. Neckel's edition of the *Prose Edda* remains the academic standard to this day.

[102] De Vries' *Altgermanische Religionsgeschichte* remains a seminal and highly regarded work in the field; he has been described as one of the greatest social scientists of his generation (Arvidsson, Stefan, *Draksjukan: Mytiska fantasier hos Tolkien, Wagner, och de Vries*, p77).

[103] von Schnurbein, *Norse Revival*, pp232-6; Jarman, *River Kings*, p125.

Norwegian fascist and Nazi collaborator Vidkun Quisling[104].

These beliefs did not remotely go away after the Second World War. They have flourished among neo-Nazi groups such as the Nordic Resistance Movement, the ecofascist movement, and neo-pagan 'Odinists' such as the 'Wolves of Vinland', the Finnish 'Soldiers of Odin', and those identifying with 'Wotanism' (Wotan being another name for Óðinn, but also standing for 'Will Of The Aryan Nation')[105].

There are multiple horrific examples of far-right shootings and mass murders with connections to Viking imagery. Anders Breivik, who killed 77 people (chiefly young socialists) in Norway in 2011, calls himself an Odinist and named his rifle, handgun, and car after Óðinn's spear, Þórr's hammer, and Óðinn's steed respectively[106]. A white supremacist heavily involved in the Ku Klux Klan who shot three people in Kansas in 2014 had previously written of Viking triumphs over the 'decadent multi-racial Roman Empire', adding that 'Valhalla does not accept N***oes. There's a sign over the pearly gates there which reads, "Whites only"'[107]. The man (and

---

[104] Jarman, *River Kings*, p125.

[105] Martyn-Hemphill, Richard, and Henrik Pryser Libell, 'Who Owns the Nazis? Pagans, Neo-Nazis and Advertisers Tussle over Symbols'; Wilson, Jason, 'Eco-fascism is Undergoing a Revival in the Fetid Culture of the Extreme Right'; Rose City Antifa, 'The Wolves of Vinland: A Fascist Countercultural "Tribe" in the Pacific Northwest'; Weber, Shannon, 'White Supremacy's Old Gods: The Far Right and Neopaganism'; Lane, David, cited in Weber, 'White Supremacy's Old Gods'.

[106] Carless, Will, 'An Ancient Nordic Religion is Inspiring White Supremacist Terror'.

[107] Cited in Weber, 'White Supremacy's Old Gods' (my asterisks).

they are almost always men) who killed two people in Portland in 2017 had referred to 'Vinland' in his online war cry and signed off his emails with various runes, which he also sported as tattoos[108]. The Islamophobic shooter who killed 51 people at two mosques in Christchurch in 2019 included an 'Odin's cross' symbol in his manifesto[109]; he also included, as did the perpetrator of the 2022 Buffalo mass shooting that killed 10 people, the phrase 'God bless you all and I hope to see you in Valhalla'[110].

More broadly, Norse-related symbols such as the Black Sun, runes, and Þórr's hammer Mjǫlnir were prominent at the 2017 'Unite the Right' rally in Charlottesville as well as tattooed on the bodies of participants in the violent storming of the Capitol by Trump supporters in January 2021[111]. There are also websites offering training courses in what it means to be a masculine Viking warrior or 'berserkr': it should be unsurprising by now that they focus on a 'very narrow definition of masculinity', that of 'heroic individuals standing alone'[112]. Norse neopaganism as a far-right starter pack thrives in certain corners of the Internet, appearing on forums and

---

[108] Acker, Lizzy, 'Jeremy Christian's Vocabulary and Related Ideas, Explained'. Vinland is an ethnic fantasy of an all-white America inspired by the name Viking explorers gave the continent.
[109] Dearden, Lizzie, 'New Zealand Attack: How Nonsensical White Genocide Conspiracy Theory Cited by Alleged Gunman is Spreading Poison Around the World'.
[110] Birkett, Tom, 'Why Far-Right Extremists Co-opt Norse Symbolism'.
[111] Birkett, Tom, 'US Capitol Riot: The Myths Behind the Tattoos Worn by "QAnon Shaman" Jake Angeli'.
[112] Dale, Roderick, 'It's Reigning Men: The Use and Abuse of Viking Masculinity'.

message boards, YouTube channels and podcasts, overlapping and intersecting with the so-called 'Manosphere', incel movements, and 'men's rights activists'[113].

It is important to note that there are, of course, plenty of self-identifying heathens continuing to worship the Norse gods who utterly disavow racist or extremist beliefs. Along with those who maintain a scholarly or merely a healthy amateur interest in the Viking Age, many heathens have tried to distance themselves from neo-Nazis[114]. However, it has been argued that this is too often treated as merely a case of shaking off an embarrassing PR problem, rather than constituting serious denunciation or active resistance[115]. It is essential that those of us who are interested in the world of Norse mythology – whatever the form that interest takes – leave **no room for doubt whatsoever** about just how unwelcome white supremacists are.

There are several methods of achieving this. Far-right narratives about the medieval world can be refuted as blatantly inaccurate fantasies in many respects. As mentioned in Chapter 1, 'viking' really refers to an activity, not an ethnicity; and far from being a homogenous ethnic group, such seafarers were far more

---

[113] Readers wishing to learn more should look no further than the superb podcast *I Don't Speak German*, which has since 2019 conducted deep-dive investigations into the disturbing world of the far right.

[114] Edwards, Catherine, 'We Can't Let Racists Re-define Viking Culture'; Fontaine, Andie Sophia, 'Pagan Chief Says Racists Co-opt Elements of Ásátru'.

[115] Sandifer, Elizabeth, 'Doing Better About Nazis'.

'multicultural and multiracial'[116] than is commonly assumed. Chapter 4, meanwhile, deals with queerness and transgressive sexual identities in the Viking Age – identities which similarly problematise the assumptions behind modern movements' rampant misogyny and homophobia. Obviously, Viking societies were far from progressive fairylands foreshadowing the future that liberals want; but nor did they remotely resemble the viciously xenophobic, rigidly insular ethno-states neo-Nazis like to imagine.

In the cultural sphere, films such as *The Northman* have done an excellent job of capturing the horrors of Vikings' toxic masculinity, while in the post-apocalyptic future of *Mad Max: Fury Road* (2015), 'Valhalla' is the promised afterlife motivating the violence of the all-male War Boys. But even though it is a truism that depiction is not endorsement, questions have been raised about to what extent such films (unintentionally) encourage and embolden these movements[117]. White nationalists admire *The Northman*, the *Lord of the Rings* films, and **Game of Thrones** for the central role played by strong white men, often as set against hordes of generic, dark-skinned monsters. The fact of their admiration does not automatically indict the creative minds behind these works, nor should it permanently sour other viewers' love for them. Clearly, it would do very little good at all – and significant harm – to ban or censor every cultural work that could possibly be distorted by extremists.

---

[116] Kim, 'White Supremacists Have Weaponized an Imaginary Viking Past'.

[117] Rose, Steve, 'Norse Code: Are White Supremacists Reading Too Much Into *The Northman*?'.

But given this context, one of the best responses available to creatives is to offer counternarratives. To make films and television (especially medievalist films and television) the far right would absolutely **hate**. To make stories which are as casually multiracial, as loudly queer, and as shamelessly un-self-serious as possible. A commonly cited example is the aforementioned *Thor: Ragnarok*. As well as its commitment to racial diversity, it features the destruction of the all-important hammer Mjǫlnir (as noted above, a widely used neo-Nazi symbol) and the obliteration of the gods' world Asgard, which is also explicitly called out as having been founded on imperialist conquest. The Asgardians become, in effect, refugees adrift in space. It does all this with lashings of quirky, irreverent humour that frequently makes fun of the Norse 'gods' themselves. The sequel, *Thor: Love and Thunder*, doubles down on this same tone, while the restored hammer is now wielded by Natalie Portman's character rather than Chris Hemsworth's. As one critic puts it, 'laughter can be a powerful antidote to the tendency to view the Middle Ages too simply'[118].

The Girl Who Died fits neatly within this tradition. It can be read as championing mockery and laughter as the most effective weapons with which to fight real-world violent ideologues. Consider: a ruthless, testosterone-obsessed military force dresses up in Viking imagery[119]. Its leader calls himself 'Odin' and in so doing distorts

---

[118] Vishnuvajjala, 'Objectivity, Impossibility and Laughter', p206.

[119] The taking of anabolic steroids such as testosterone has already been discussed as a means of appearing more masculine. The same impulse animates the far right's anger at, and rejection of, what they perceive as emasculating substances such as soy milk (Sommer, Will, 'How "Soy Boy" Became the Far Right's Favorite

the true spirit of a slippery and mercurial trickster-god who is not just associated with warfare but also with poetry, queer and shamanistic magic, and healing. His Mire legions are a bastardised, cracked-mirror reflection of Valkyries – a hyper-masculine iteration of the mythological female figures who choose the best warriors to accompany them to 'Valhalla'. The version of Norse mythology offered up by these self-serious warmongers is explicitly exposed as a sham, an empty echo of a real belief system. The Mire are absolutely dangerous enough to do real, lethal damage, but the fearsome reputation they cultivate is significantly overstated – almost as though they sound more intimidating in their manifestos than they are in real life. Ultimately, what sends them packing is documented footage of their running scared from a silly and unconvincing wooden puppet, footage the characters themselves recognise as 'really funny' and 'hilarious', set to possibly the most famous piece of music for accompanying outlandish farce. The fear of being exposed to ridicule, the very **threat** of apotropaic laughter rather than the laughter itself, is enough to keep them at bay. No wonder the 12th Doctor tells his successor to follow in his footsteps by laughing hard.

This particular resonance clarifies why a new race, the Mire, were created for the story rather than reusing an existing monster, the Sontarans. One might fairly ask why the production team went to such an effort when the Sontarans are already a very good fit: they are a clear pastiche of buffoonish, vainglorious militarism, and no

---

New Insult'). There is a comparable level of insecurity in quaffing testosterone so as to appear manly and spurning drinks with a high phytoestrogen content so as not to be thought effeminate.

additional expense would be needed for costumes or prosthetics. They even have previous form when it comes to comically excessive warmongering in a medieval setting[120]. So close in function are the two that the Sontarans practically haunt the concept of the Mire: cut dialogue would have had Clara ask what the Mire's weakness was and explicitly drawing a comparison with the Sontarans' probic vents at the back of their necks[121]; and the photo novelisation namedrops them, instead of the Velosians, as the Doctor and Clara's opponents from the adventure immediately preceding this one[122]. But for all the ways they fit, there are no specific Viking inflections to the Sontarans – they are a satire of broader militaristic jingoism as opposed to a far-right movement fixated on Viking motifs. It might therefore have been a distracting case of over-signification to stir that additional element into the existing mix.

This message offered by *The Girl Who Died* has its limitations, however, and they should be recognised. The story does a strong job of capturing certain key aspects of far-right movements: violence, militarism, ridiculous Viking cosplay, toxic masculinity, and latent homophobia borne out of insecurity. It says practically nothing, however, about white supremacy or racialised hatred[123]. Given that a racialised view of the world is at the core of modern

---

[120] For more on Sontarans and militarism in the Middle Ages, see Kilburn, Matthew, *The Black Archive #24: The Time Warrior*.

[121] TCH #81, p102.

[122] Rollason, *Doctor Who: The Girl Who Died*, p2.

[123] It says nothing about antisemitism either, but that would have been an admittedly difficult inclusion in a story set centuries before Judaism arrived in Norway.

fascist and neo-Nazi ideology, this is a significant flaw, to say the least. There is perhaps something pointed and ethnically essentialist in the fact that the Mire drink testosterone specifically distilled from a white Germanic people, given that this is a repeated choice on their part (as is made clear in the deleted scene, they have made several visits to the village in the past). And, of course, 'Odin' greets the Vikings as '[his] people' when trying to convince them that he is a legitimate manifestation of their religion's sovereign deity. But for the most part this aspect simply is not explored or even considered in the episode at all.

Together with the fact that the episode's entire cast is white[124], this results in the unintentionally awkward subtext of a homestead of white Germanic people – exactly the sort of society the far right have historically revered – fending off grotesque invaders who are not like them but are encroaching on their land and resources. To some extent, the 'Us vs Them' division of two white leads and Viking villagers against an army of alien Others is unfortunate. However, any attempt to read the episode as endorsing this view stumbles into incoherence: the Mire are explicitly coded within the

---

[124] This is largely 'historically accurate' insofar as we can judge these things – although various other films and TV series set in medieval Scandinavia **have** cast actors of colour, usually to show how Viking trade routes brought them into contact with a wide variety of cultures across the Mediterranean and North Africa. This is even the case for two of the earliest such films, although Sandpiper in *The Vikings* is the archetypal deaf-and-mute slave/strongman, and, despite featuring a black Viking, *The Norseman* (1978) is racially dicey in other respects, pitting valiant Scandinavians against aggressive, unintelligible Native Americans who are very much coded as 'Other'.

text as cut from the same cloth as the Vikings themselves, merely writ large on a more cosmic canvas. It would take quite a distorted reach to see in this unambiguous mockery of figures who resemble the Odinist brand of neo-Nazism even an accidental depiction of far-right talking points.

There are, arguably, other ways in which *The Girl Who Died*'s politics fall short. It is pretty obviously insufficient to rely wholly on humour and silliness as weapons against rising neo-Nazism. The far right are frequently ridiculous, yes, and they are absolutely worth mocking; but they are also terrifying. The **feeling** of terror can, perhaps, be defused by the relief of laughter; but real-world acts of terror cannot. As the saying goes, Weimar cabaret did not prevent the rise of Hitler. You cannot stop the gunman in front of you through the power of satire. Even the assumption that an incriminating or embarrassing recording can stop a far-right movement in its tracks has a kind of well-meaning but naïve optimism about it, given that such methods have since been routinely dismissed as 'fake news', doctored footage, or 'deep fakes' in the real world.

At some point, though, someone writing 38,000 words on a 45-minute episode of **Doctor Who** has to admit that there might be such a thing as taking the programme too seriously. It would be unreasonable and uncharitable to fault *The Girl Who Died* for not presenting a pinpoint-accurate commentary of the Odinist branch of the far right, or for not coming up with a politically nuanced praxis for dismantling such movements. To some readers this may sound like a copout: why subject the story to rigorous analysis over its evoking such subject matter, if only to offer the 'it's only children's television' defence when it does not go far enough? Is that not trying to have it both ways? Perhaps it is. It is the paradox of art that it both does and does not make things happen. It can express or reinforce a worldview, preach to the converted, provoke the comfortable, or rile up its intended targets. But it is, as the Doctor puts it, 'nothing without an audience'[125] – without people to receive, digest, and be inspired by its ideas.

The 'epic theatre' of Bertolt Brecht, which challenged people to go out and change the world, was never intended to be sufficient on its own; rather, plays were to serve as catalysts for people to take radical action. If art is to have any material force at all as a springboard for activism, it must be merely a part of a wide range of acts. This episode is ultimately nothing more than another brick in the wall of antifascism and cannot hope to shoulder any more weight than the brick immediately above it. Yet what is any wall, even the most robust, but a multitude of bricks?

[125] *Heaven Sent* (2015).

CHAPTER 3: ÓÐINN-AS-TRICKSTER AND WAYS OF VIEWING

'Dr Who isn't a scientist. He's a wizard.'

[William Hartnell][126]

At around the six-minute mark, *The Girl Who Died* sees two opposing figures – the Doctor and the unnamed leader of the Mire – claim, in quick succession, to be the Norse god Odin. In an irony wholly in keeping with the episode's interest in perception versus reality, the latter's disguise as the deity is ostensibly far more convincing, but the former bears a closer resemblance in many ways to Óðinn as he is depicted in mythological sources. This pair of claims reveals a great deal about how the episode uses Norse mythology within the context of the fundamental ideological battle at its core. This chapter examines the numerous compelling similarities between the Doctor and Óðinn, similarities which allow the story's motifs of sight and perception to come into sharper focus. These in turn lead to an exploration of 'true' versus 'fake' faces in the episode's juxtaposition of the Doctor and the villainous 'Odin', demonstrating why it is so fitting that the answer to the question 'Who frowned me this face?' occurs here[127].

3.1: 'Have You Met Odin? Do You Know What Odin Looks Like?'

Why might the Doctor choose to impersonate Odin specifically, rather than another Norse god such as Freyr or Þórr? His choice is

---

[126] 'Spaceman Bill is Down to Earth', *Reveille*, January 7-13, 1965.
[127] *Deep Breath* (2014).

far from random; indeed, there is a long history of comparisons between the two. Setting to one side Hartnell's categorising of his character as a 'wizard' and other nods in this direction over the years[128], the Doctor was first explicitly compared to the wizard-like god Óðinn as early as 1988, even before the seventh Doctor's Odinic qualities manifested in TV stories drawing on Norse mythology such as *The Greatest Show in the Galaxy* and *The Curse of Fenric*, not to mention the appearance of explicitly Odinic imagery in the novel *Timewyrm: Revelation* (1991). Writing that the Doctor 'is the best possible example of the shaman, the wizard-king, the wise magician', James L Hodge grants that any comparisons with the Arthurian Merlin are 'not too far off'[129] but sees Norse mythology as providing an even more apt analogue:

> 'the **most potent** wizard, king of the gods, master-by-force-of-knowledge-and-intellect is none other than Odin, chief of the Norse gods [...] Odin has concentrated on mastery of lore, acquisition of knowledge, and a forewarning of the future. He rules more by the power of what he knows, and can therefore do, than by his physical power [...] Just so, the [Doctor] confronts opponent after opponent whose

---

[128] E.g., Ben Jackson bluffing that the Doctor is a wizard in *The Smugglers* (1966) episode 2, or the description of the Doctor as 'the great wizard Quiquaequod' in *The Dæmons* (1971) episode 4. He is also regularly described as a 'magician' in *The Time Warrior*, a story to which *The Girl Who Died* bears some resemblance.

[129] Amusingly, Hodge's article appeared around 18 months before the revelation that a future incarnation of the Doctor was fated to become Merlin in *Battlefield* (1989). For more on the Doctor's connections with Merlin, see Purser-Hallard, Philip, *The Black Archive #34: Battlefield*.

arrogant plans go aground on some esoteric reef of the [Doctor]'s immense, technical knowledge'.[130]

Various critics have since noted a clearly pagan-influenced approach towards the seventh Doctor taken by writers such as Paul Cornell, or the ways in which the Doctor resembles Óðinn more generally[131]. The Doctor's surprising affinity for the Vikings' pagan beliefs was even originally nodded to in *The Girl Who Died*, in a sequence at the end in which he was made 'an honorary Jarl' of the village, explicitly described as 'the first community he had ever felt part of'[132].

It might seem a little odd to so closely align a Norse god and an Enlightenment figure who is (at least superficially) an arch-rationalist and a scientist, especially one who is not averse to debunking belief in the supernatural or divine in their role as 'the enemy of myth'[133]. On the other hand, such a description reduces the Doctor to just one of their many aspects. The broader question of whether the Doctor is more of a scientist or a wizard is outside the scope of this book. However, it might be most accurate to follow Rafer's assertion that the character synthesises science and

---

[130] Hodge, James L, 'New Bottles – Old Wine: The Persistence of the Heroic Figure in the Mythology of Television Science Fiction and Fantasy', *Journal of Popular Culture* 21:4, p40 (emphasis in original).

[131] E.g., Wiggins, Anna, 'Odin and the Doctor'; Charles, Alec, *Out of Time: The Deaths and Resurrections of Doctor Who*, pp173-78; Sandifer, *TARDIS Eruditorum Vol 6*, pp128-30.

[132] TCH #81, p90.

[133] Rafer, David, 'Mythic identity in **Doctor Who**', in Butler, ed, *Time and Relative Dissertations in Space*, p129.

myth by maintaining 'a kind of duality between [their] irrational, intuitive nature and the dominance of reason and rationalism', becoming as a result a 'multifaceted mythic hero'[134].

As Hodge outlines above, there is certainly some common ground between the Doctor and Óðinn: they are both powerful, mythical figures of great wisdom whose fundamental strength derives from sharpness of intellect rather than physical prowess. There is, however, more to the comparison than this, and more detailed analysis yields a sizeable amount of overlap, in areas which illuminate the juxtaposition of both 'fake Odins' in *The Girl Who Died*.

Assessing the similarities between the two is immediately complicated by Óðinn's erratic, fluctuating nature, a nature which contains multitudes (as Anna Wiggins puts it, he is 'bigger on the inside'[135]). That said, that mercurial changeability in itself constitutes a similarity with a protagonist who can completely alter their body, gender, and aspects of their personality. Both Norse mythology and the mythos of **Doctor Who** form incomplete and self-contradictory pictures told across a wide variety of sources, generating multiple different portrayals of both Óðinn and the Doctor, leaving the distinct impression that neither can be fully known. One identifiable constant is Óðinn's depiction as the ruler of the Æsir, the Norse gods[136]: this crucial position within the

---

[134] Rafer, 'Mythic identity in **Doctor Who**', p134.
[135] Wiggins, 'Odin and the Doctor'.
[136] See e.g., Snorri Sturluson in Faulkes, Anthony, ed and trans, *Edda: Prologue and Gylfaginning*, pp8-9: 'highest and most ancient of all gods [...] he lives throughout all ages and rules all his kingdom

pantheon marks him out as a sovereign deity akin to Zeus/Jupiter in the Greco-Roman mythos[137]. In this respect he is the powerful leader of a cosmic hierarchy in a way that is never really true of the Doctor, who, while occasionally ascending to the office of President of Gallifrey or of Earth, is pretty consistently shown to flee from such authority and responsibility[138].

Indeed, when it comes to wielding power over others, 'Odin' makes a far more convincing 'ruler of the gods' than the Doctor: compare the former's appearing in the heavens and leading an army of formidable warriors with the latter's throwing a yo-yo and assembling a rag-tag bunch of distinctly unimposing villagers. However, it is not hard to see the Doctor's position as a member – however renegade – of an elite society of beings who are 'functionally immortal' and who created, or certainly upheld, the Laws of Time as echoing the Æsir's own cosmic dominance[139]. The

---

and governs all things great and small'. Even though Snorri's 13th-century depiction of Óðinn is in part influenced by the omnipotent God of monotheistic Christianity, it remains the case even in older sources such as the *Poetic Edda* that 'Óðinn dominates everything' (Turville-Petre, Gabriel, *Nine Norse Studies*, p1).

[137] Note that the Doctor has taken on the mantle of Zeus' identity at least once before, in *The Myth Makers* (1965).

[138] See *The Deadly Assassin* (1976), *The Invasion of Time* (1978), *The Five Doctors* (1983), *Death in Heaven* (2014), *The Zygon Invasion* (2015) and *The Pyramid at the End of the World* (2017). In *The Face of Evil* (1977), the Doctor's personality has become imprinted on the supercomputer Xoanon, which is then revered as a god. For more on why this situation does not go terribly well, see Rodebaugh, Thomas L, *The Black Archive #27: The Face of Evil*.

[139] Various episodes suggest this, but perhaps the Doctor's declaration, in *The Waters of Mars* (2009), that his 'people' were

Time Lords and their technology have been compared to gods, after all, while Óðinn and his brothers in effect set time in motion by placing the stars in their 'courses' in the sky, 'by means of [which] days were distinguished and also the count of years'[140].

Óðinn possesses a number of uglier, more uncomfortable traits, many of which seem at first glance to have little to do with the Doctor but, upon closer reflection, prove disquietingly applicable to both figures. In order to form the universe, Óðinn kills the giant Ymir and fashions material reality out of the corpse's remains as well as drowning almost the entire race of 'jǫtnar' or giants[141]. This would hardly be considered typical Doctor behaviour, although they, too, have destroyed entire populated worlds, been charged with genocide in a court, and spent several lifetimes believing that they wiped out their own people[142].

Within the fiction, this last act was the culmination of the Last Great Time War, a conflict during which the Doctor – despite renouncing that name – served on the frontlines, in another echo of one of Óðinn's less savoury aspects. The god is commonly associated with war, military success, and warriors: he is portrayed as being able to blind or deafen his enemies on the battlefield[143],

---

once 'in charge of' such laws is the most explicit.

[140] *Underworld* (1978) episode 1, *Boom Town* (2005); Snorri Sturluson, *Edda*, p12.

[141] Snorri Sturluson, *Edda*, p11.

[142] *Remembrance of the Daleks* (1988); 'Terror of the Vervoids' (*The Trial of a Time Lord* episodes 9 to 12, 1986); *The End of the World* (2005), *Dalek* (2005), et al, although *The Day of the Doctor* alters his past timeline.

[143] Snorri Sturluson, *Heimskringla Vol 1*, p10.

invites fallen warriors to dine with him in Valhǫll who then fight each other on a daily basis[144], and inspires modern-day masculinist cults of Odinists, as we have seen. It is in this sense that 'Odin' most closely imitates the deity, in his explicit invitation to the village's 'mightiest warriors' to 'feast with [him] tonight in the halls of Valhalla' and in his overt delight in warfare. The Doctor, by contrast, is not typically portrayed as martial or militaristic, embracing peaceful solutions over warfare wherever possible and only in exceptional circumstances (e.g., in the Time War) fighting as a soldier in an army. The previous season had established Capaldi's 12th Doctor in particular as having a strong antagonism towards soldiers, especially Clara's now-deceased boyfriend Danny Pink.

Nevertheless, 21st-century **Doctor Who** in particular presents the character as being widely perceived by others as a warrior, despite not self-identifying as such. The Pandorica is built to imprison 'the greatest warrior in history', which turns out to be the Doctor; his name comes to mean 'mighty warrior' to the people of the Gamma Forests; and he admits that 'thinking like a warrior' has 'always been [his] problem'[145]. The character is also portrayed, on occasion, as a figure who 'take[s] ordinary people and fashion[s] them into weapons'[146], with many of their companions taking on military roles after departing, which echoes Óðinn welcoming the Einherjar, chosen warriors, to Valhǫll. In *The Girl Who Died* the Doctor spends time training inexperienced villagers in swordplay,

---

[144] Snorri Sturluson, *Edda*, pp32-34.

[145] *The Pandorica Opens*; *A Good Man Goes to War* (2011); *Empress of Mars* (2017).

[146] *Journey's End* (2008). See also 'Is that what you did to her? Turned her into a soldier?' in *The Sontaran Stratagem* (2008).

however reluctantly (and unsuccessfully), and his characteristically valiant defence of the story's underdogs resembles the mythological Óðinn's capricious tendency to grant victory to the seemingly undeserving or 'faint-hearted'[147].

Furthermore, Óðinn is an explicitly patriarchal figure. As mentioned in the introduction, his most famous moniker is 'All-Father', and he is described not just as ruler of the other gods but also as their father – which, while probably not literally true of the entire pantheon, does apply to notables such as Baldr and Þórr[148]. It is little surprise, then, that this Father-of-Everything's virility makes him 'the **manliest** god of warriors'[149], which is certainly how the testosterone-swigging 'Odin' wishes to be perceived.

Much as one would expect from a patriarch wielding ultimate authority, Óðinn's gender politics are frequently abhorrent, and there are stories of his seducing and even raping giantesses or goddesses to get what he wants[150]. It is clearly out of the question

---

[147] *Lokasenna*, stanza 22 (Larrington, *The Poetic Edda*, p84).

[148] It is perhaps best to understand Óðinn as occupying the position of a father figure towards other gods than as literally fathering them all; this certainly seems to be how Snorri understands it – 'mighty though the other gods are, yet they all submit to him **like** children to their father' (*Edda*, p21, emphasis mine).

[149] Solli, Brit, 'Queering the Cosmology of the Vikings: A Queer Analysis of the Cult of Odin and "Holy White Stones"', *Journal of Homosexuality* 54:1/2, p195 (emphasis in original).

[150] Snorri Sturluson, *Edda*, pp62-3; Kormákr Ögmundarson, *Sigurðardrápa*, stanza 3, cited by Snorri Sturluson in *Edda*, p68; Grammaticus, Saxo in Elton, Oliver, trans, *The Nine Books of the Danish History of Saxo Grammaticus in Two Volumes*, pp192-6; John Lindow (in *Norse Mythology*, p205) speculates that Óðinn's

for the protagonist of a family show to be even hinted at as engaging in such acts; there is, however, significant precedent for seeing the Doctor as patriarchal – in their male incarnations at least. Indeed, a tendency in that direction is specifically critiqued throughout Peter Capaldi's tenure, especially during Series 9, in which Clara Oswald calls out his self-proclaimed 'duty of care' in *Under the Lake* (2015) and *Hell Bent* (2015). When he restates that he has this duty towards her in *The Girl Who Died*, Clara retorts 'no, you don't, because I never asked for that,' much as she will with yet more vehemence in the series finale. The patriarchal tendencies common to both are even more closely associated when the Doctor-as-Odin adopts the tone of a disappointed father figure and chastises the Norsemen with the words 'I am very, very cross with you. I am very disappointed'[151].

In a number of ways, then, both the Doctor and 'Odin' echo Óðinn's more potentially problematic elements – on the battlefield, in their privilege, and in their assumptions that they know what is best for others (particularly women). In the case of the Doctor, these more distasteful Odinic elements are the regular subject of explicit criticism and exhortations to do better. However, a yet stronger resemblance to most characterisations of the Doctor can be found in Óðinn's much more compellingly likable depiction as a cunning, eccentric trickster.

The Trickster is a noted Jungian archetype, one which has been

---

sexual relationship with Jǫrð was not willing on her part.

[151] A phrase which, in its first part at least, echoes Steven Moffat's cliffhanger resolution to *The Empty Child / The Doctor Dances* (2005).

applied to both Óðinn and the Doctor by those comparing the two[152]. Even for those who harbour a healthy scepticism towards the universality of Jungian archetypes, Alec Charles' 'post-Jungian' approach is nevertheless worthwhile for the way it views such archetypes 'not as immutably universal but as icons generated by cultural traditions'[153]. Key features of Tricksters (sometimes categorised alongside clowns, discussed in Chapter 2) include a penchant for disruptive humour, an ability to transgress or transcend boundaries, and a liminal position both within, and outside of, cultural normativity. A particularly apt definition has, in fact, been provided by **Doctor Who** itself: 'the clown-stroke-jester is a familiar figure, anthropologically speaking. He defuses a potential source of conflict through mockery and ridicule.'[154]

Although the principal 'trickster god' of the Norse pantheon is a different figure, the morally murky Loki, Óðinn nonetheless displays notable Trickster-like traits which equally apply to the Doctor: despite coming from immense privilege, both are capricious wanderers who are associated with healing, quests for knowledge, abilities that border on the magical, and upending established orders or transgressing rules. In this respect, the Mire 'Odin' is almost nothing like the deity whose identity he assumes,

---

[152] Rafer, 'Mythic identity in **Doctor Who**', p124; Tulloch, John, and Manuel Alvarado, *The Unfolding Text*, pp270-79; Sandifer, *TARDIS Eruditorum Vol 6*, pp128-29; Charles, Alec, 'Three Characters in Search of an Archetype: Aspects of the Trickster and the *Flâneur* in the Characterizations of Sherlock Holmes, Gregory House, and Doctor Who', *Journal of Popular Television* 1:1, pp83-102.

[153] Charles, 'Three Characters in Search of an Archetype', p84.

[154] *Kinda* (1982) episode 3.

whereas the Doctor fits every one of these categories, right down to flouting rigidly defined conventions; note that in *The Girl Who Died* he breaks the same 'rules of life and death' he criticised the Fisher King for merely 'bending' only a week before[155].

The resemblance is, in fact, even stronger now than it might have seemed to medieval worshippers of Óðinn. While some medieval Christian sources treat the god as a sinister 'chief of devils'[156], others such as the 13th-century *Ynglinga Saga* and *Gylfaginning* appear keen neither to allow paganism to contradict Christian beliefs nor to invalidate Norse tradition. The resultant compromises suggested that Óðinn was more of a powerful mortal wizard (and historical earthly king) than a god per se, but still identified him as capable of roughly the same acts of magic and quasi-divine power as the pagan sources had[157]. These revisions are what is known as euhemeristic: assuming that mythological figures were inspired by real historical individuals. In some ways, this later interpretation brings Óðinn closer to most conceptions of the Doctor (and fittingly so, given the Doctor's own tendency within the fiction to demystify gods), coding both figures more along the lines of mysterious, transgressive magicians than universe-ruling

---

[155] *Before the Flood* (2015).

[156] Mitchell, Stephen A, '"Nú Gef ek Þik Óðni": Attitudes toward Odin in the Mythical-Heroic sagas', in Louis-Jensen, Jonna, Christopher Sanders, and Peter Springborg, eds, *The Sixth International Saga Conference, 28.7-28.8 1985: Workshop papers I-II*, p777.

[157] Snorri Sturluson, *Heimskringla Vol 1*, pp6-11, and *Edda*, p3. In Saxo Grammaticus, *Danish History*, p110, Óðinn is 'credited over all Europe with the honour, which was **false**, of godhead' (emphasis mine).

deities.

Óðinn has been called 'the arch-magician of Norse myth', while Peter Capaldi's 12th Doctor is often compared to a magician in both apparel and behaviour, even on one occasion in an episode title[158]. The visual parallel is made still more striking through regular depictions of the former as a man with grey-white hair. After echoing Clarke's Third Law by telling Clara that 'to the primitive mind, advanced technology can seem like magic'[159] as a rationale for how his yo-yo will impress the Vikings, the Doctor adroitly frees himself from his manacles and promptly gives an incredulous Clara the same explanation – 'magic'. Even if handwaved away as the Doctor reusing escapology tips he has picked up from the recurrently name-dropped Houdini[160], the joke here, of course, is that the 21st-century companion and audience identification member is equally in awe of his sorcerous abilities as the medieval raiders (if anything, more so).

The Doctor may not have a sonic screwdriver in *The Girl Who Died*, having replaced it temporarily with his sonic sunglasses, but his normal-service multi-function device of choice only adds to the magical undertones. It may pose as a scientific instrument, but it is also a long, thin, rod-like tool that arbitrarily makes all number of supernatural things happen depending on the power of narrative

---

[158] Evans, DAH, Introduction to *Hávamál*, p33; *Time Heist* (2014), *Last Christmas*, 'The Doctor's Meditation' (2015) and *The Magician's Apprentice*.

[159] This Law is also referenced in *The Pirate Planet* (1978), *Battlefield*, and *The Witchfinders* (2018).

[160] *Planet of the Spiders* (1974) episode 5 and on several occasions since.

convenience. It is rather fitting that fans taking umbrage with the device's hyper-powered capabilities in modern **Doctor Who** criticise it as resembling 'a magic wand' – it practically is one[161]. Similarly, a particularly well-known phrase from 20th-century **Doctor Who** – in this form 'reversing the polarity of the neutron flow', though it appears in various permutations over the years[162] – is used in *The Girl Who Died* by the Doctor and then immediately undercut by the revelation that he 'bet[s] that means something, it sounds great.' In other words, for all the phrase's pseudo-scientific trappings (and for all the reverence in which it is held by fans), the character using it actively recognises that it is little more than a set of words which help move a given plot mechanic forward. Language holding a power that is practically mystical: what is that but an incantation or a spell?

Other similarities abound between the Doctor and Óðinn. The latter is not merely the god of war, after all, but also of poetry and 'all secret wisdom'[163]. While the Doctor's translation of the baby's speech in *The Girl Who Died* has been explicitly compared to 'the metre and style of Norse poetry'[164], the notion of the Doctor harbouring 'terrible, dangerous secret[s] that must never be

---

[161] It has also been described as such in the programme, in *Love & Monsters* (2006), *Robot of Sherwood*, *Thin Ice* (2017), and *The Witchfinders*.

[162] It first appears in *Terror of the Autons* (1971) episode 4 as 'change the polarity', and frequently thereafter in the more famous form, including multiple appearances in Moffat scripts.

[163] Turville-Petre, Gabriel, *Nine Norse Studies*, p1.

[164] Burk and Smith?, *Who Is the Doctor 2*, p179. This assertion will be examined in the Appendix.

told'[165] is a long-standing one that recurs throughout the series, from the secret Lady Peinforte threatens to uncover in *Silver Nemesis* (1988) all the way through to the secrets others seek to get out of him in *The Name of the Doctor* (2013) and *Heaven Sent* (2015). One such secret is the Doctor's real name, although it has been observed that throughout his wanderings he has garnered 'many names', among them Doctor Who, John Smith, Theta Sigma, Karshtakavaar (the Oncoming Storm), Ka Faraq Gatri (the Destroyer of Worlds), the Imp of the Pandorica, the Beast of Trenzalore, the Shadow of the Valeyard, and the Last Tree of Garsennon[166]. Óðinn is similarly known for having myriad names, including Alfǫðr, Báleyg, Gangleri, Hangagoð, Fimbultýr and Bǫlverkr; one study totted up 169 such aliases in the extant literature[167]. In both cases the accumulated impression is of a figure of slippery and mercurial identity adopting and shedding guises at will.

Time travel is also frequently referred to in **Doctor Who** as a 'secret' which those without it wish to possess[168] – and even in this respect the Doctor and Óðinn have something in common. The god

---

[165] *The Wedding of River Song*.

[166] *Twice Upon a Time*. Such aliases or titles are first given on television in *The War Machines* (1966) episode 1, *The Wheel in Space* (1968) episode 2, *The Armageddon Factor* (1979) episode 5, *The Parting of the Ways* (2005), *Journey's End*, and *Twice Upon a Time* respectively. The last designation on this list is of particular interest, given that various Old Norse words for 'tree' are used in kennings to describe human(oid)s, typically men. Kennings will be discussed in the Appendix.

[167] Falk, Hjalmar, *Odensheite*.

[168] *The War Games* (1969) episode 5 and on several occasions since.

is a perpetual traveller known for his wandering far and wide, including to others of the Nine Worlds in Norse cosmology such as the land of the dead – a form of travel that arguably navigates both space and time. Throughout these travels, one constant is Óðinn's quest for different kinds of knowledge, often gaining it from various other mythical figures he encounters. Critics have called Óðinn both a 'repository' and the 'source' of the world's knowledge; throughout the Odinic wisdom contest *Vafþrúðnismál,* having widely travelled is explicitly linked to wisdom[169]. This is also evocative of this particular Doctor, who 'hate[s] not knowing' and says of one obsession 'I have to know!'[170] More intriguingly still, Óðinn has been described as possessing a ship, Skíðbladnir, that contains multitudes within a small exterior, which 'sailed over high seas, but [...] could be folded together like a cloth'[171], in what sounds uncannily like a centuries-old description of the TARDIS's dimensional transcendentalism. In short, Óðinn is a peripatetic wanderer from a privileged race which wields mastery over time, journeying in a ship which is bigger within than without. There is perhaps no human deity the Doctor more closely resembles.

---

[169] Byock, Jesse, introduction to *Prose Edda*, p xviii; Auld, Richard L, 'The Psychological and Mythic Unity of the God, Óðinn', *Numen: International Review for the History of Religions* 23, p146; *Vafþrúðnismál*, stanza 3 and frequently thereafter, especially Vafþrúðnir's declaration in stanza 43 (Larrington, *The Poetic Edda*, pp37-46).

[170] *Time Heist*; *Listen* (2014).

[171] Snorri Sturluson, *Heimskringla Vol 1*, p10. Conventionally, the ship belongs to a different deity, Freyr, but it is notable that Snorri here ascribes it to Óðinn. Ashildr originally made a similar comparison in the sixth draft of *The Girl Who Died* (TCH #81, p98).

Lastly, the Doctor and Óðinn are both associated with healing. In Óðinn's case this appears pictorially on various bracteates (Germanic gold medals) and in other visual depictions, but the most textually explicit example occurs in the Second Merseburg Charm. Written in ninth- or 10th-century Old High German and referring to Wodan (cognate for Óðinn), the charm describes how the god uses a magical incantation to heal an injury, fusing bones back together and repairing limbs[172]. Not only is there the obvious association between 'Doctor' and 'healing', an association made explicit in the programme itself[173], but the Doctor reproduces Óðinn's medical intervention in *The Girl Who Died* when he uses Mire technology to 'repair' the dead Ashildr. The Viking girl's return to life at the Doctor's hand is conveyed through her sudden intake of breath, recalling not just the earlier resurrections of another immortal, Jack Harkness, but also Óðinn's specific mythological role in granting 'breath' to the very earliest humans, Askr and Embla[174]. By doing this for Ashildr, the Doctor effectively supplants Óðinn; the intervention 'makes the Doctor, in a sense, her (all)father'[175].

Given the pre-existing parallels between these two figures, then, it is an eminently sensible choice to have the Doctor pose as Óðinn upon encountering Vikings. The Mire leader's claim to be Odin might be superficially more credible, but the episode illustrates on

---

[172] See Lindow, *Norse Mythology*, pp227-28.
[173] *A Good Man Goes to War*.
[174] *Vǫluspá*, stanza 18 (Larrington, *The Poetic Edda*, p6). The singular of Æsir, 'áss' or 'god', which forms the first syllable of Ashildr's name, even has as its cognate the Sanskrit 'ásu', meaning 'spirit/life force'.
[175] Kashevsky, 'Folk Heroes and the Doctor'.

multiple occasions that the Doctor is far less of a 'false Odin' than his opponent. This raises questions about the extent to which we can trust our own eyes, questions in which the story is fundamentally invested.

3.2: 'All Too Easy to Feed in a New Reality'

Visual perception is a recurring obsession throughout Moffat's tenure as showrunner of **Doctor Who**: how perspectives can be altered, how we make sense of what we see, or how our own sight can be weaponised against us. This manifests most visibly, as it were, in the Weeping Angels and the Silence; whether or not such foes are being observed is crucial to their abilities and to the act of opposing them. It is a wider theme, however: in **Doctor Who** from 2010-17, and especially in Moffat's scripts, dream sequences in which the visual world cannot be trusted are commonplace, as are monstrous manifestations of the eye motif, sequences hinging entirely upon a character's subjective visual perspective, and strikingly memorable eye close-ups more generally[176].

This is particularly true of Series 9, nowhere better exemplified than in the way the sonic sunglasses introduced in the series opener shift the centre of the Doctor's technical wizardry from a hand tool to the power of his gaze. *Sleep No More* is perhaps the

---

[176] Examples of each of these categories include: *Flesh and Stone* (2010), *Amy's Choice* (2010), *Last Christmas,* and *The Zygon Inversion* (2015); the Atraxi, the Eknodine, the Gangers' wall of eyes, and the Teselecta; *The Eleventh Hour* (2010), *A Christmas Carol, Asylum of the Daleks* (2012), *The Crimson Horror* (2013), and *Sleep No More*; *The Rings of Akhaten* (2013), *Kill the Moon* (2014), and *The Pilot* (2017).

most obvious example of the programme experimenting with visual perception and focussing on the act of viewing, using not only point of view camerawork as an homage to the found footage genre but also developing its threat out of the sleep dust that builds up in the corner of the human eye. *Under the Lake* and *Before the Flood* (2015) give us ancient writing which works its way through individuals' eyes into their minds, as well as the ghosts' cavernous sockets where their eyes should be – symbolic of their having been reduced to mere vessels for a single message, no longer permitted vision of their own. The series opener's handmines evoke the evil eye motif of antiquity, while Davros claims he wishes to see the sun again with his own eyes. Later in the series, shapeshifting Zygons make it harder to spot the difference between friend and foe, Clara uses winking as a means of communication when the Zygon Bonnie has taken her form, and London's Trap Street is hidden from view through a 'cloaking device' which 'normalises everything you see'[177] in a manner akin to previously established perception filters. Even *The Woman Who Lived* (2015) sees Ashildr and the Doctor searching for an alien artefact known as the Eyes of Hades.

Given this context, it would be surprising if *The Girl Who Died* did not follow suit in some way, and as Jane Campbell has illustrated, it does indeed feature a plethora of 'eye imagery'. The motif is foregrounded right from the opening shot – an extreme close-up of Clara's right eye, upside-down, as she drifts through space – and through the fact that the Doctor is able to locate her when she describes the stars and nebulae in her frame of vision. Script and

---

[177] *Face the Raven* (2015).

direction imbue sight with significance from the very beginning; the final shot similarly places Ashildr's expressive eyes in the centre of the frame where they command attention. Throughout the rest of the episode, director Ed Bazalgette also gives us close-ups of the eye of a carved wooden prow and the red slit on the eyepatch worn by 'Odin', as well as a medium close-up of the 'rather Cyclopean'[178] single slits on the Mire warriors' helmets which serve as their 'eyes'. The viewer is also granted several glimpses of the Mire's vision filtered through the technology of their helmets while they survey the villagers (moreover, the creation of a 'crude sock puppet' to assess the Mire's capacity for facial recognition was part of the earliest episode outlines)[179].

The focus on sight and perception is not created solely by Bazalgette's camerawork but also by the use of specific props, with both the Doctor's sonic sunglasses and the virtual reality eyepatch worn by 'Odin' playing significant roles in the plot. Mathieson and Moffat's dialogue similarly draws attention to this persistent motif: the Viking nicknamed 'Heidi' closes his eyes because he struggles with 'the sight of blood', while the Doctor tells 'Odin' that he's just experienced the world 'through the eyes of a storyteller' and later lists Clara's **eyes** – and, implicitly, her way of seeing the world – as an important attribute of hers alongside her 'never giving up', her anger and her kindness.

This litany of creative decisions is far from random, and indeed perfectly aligns with the episode's evocation of the mythological

---

[178] Campbell, Jane, 'The Eyes Have It (**Doctor Who**: *The Girl Who Died*)'.
[179] TCH #81, p88.

Óðinn. The god's aforementioned capacity for wisdom is understood in Norse-Icelandic sources to stem from his having first sacrificed an eye; by (partially) losing the privilege of physical sight, he is rewarded with greater spiritual and epistemological insight, or 'vision'[180]. Snorri records in *Gylfaginning* that Óðinn 'saw over all worlds and every man's activity and understood everything he saw'[181], drawing on the familiar connection between sight and wisdom that still exists in plenty of English idioms. 'Odin' wearing a virtual reality patch over one eye is a nod to both this mythological sacrifice and to conventional depictions of the god wearing an eyepatch, also echoed in Clara wearing half of the Doctor's sonic sunglasses over one eye. Additionally, the Doctor will lose **his** power of sight in Mathieson's next script, *Oxygen* (2017), beginning a mini-arc spanning three episodes of Series 10. The following two stories place emphasis on the ways in which his blindness is a hindrance, but in *Oxygen* itself the newly blinded Doctor is able to see more deeply into the true rot at the heart of 'capitalism in space'.

One of several sources of knowledge upon which Óðinn relies is the head of Mímir, detached from the body of another, lesser god yet still able to provide the Alfǫðr with wisdom when he requests it (indeed, it appears to have been Mímir to whom Óðinn sacrificed his eye)[182]. Although there is no equivalent in *The Girl Who Died*, it

---

[180] *Vǫluspá*, stanza 29 (Larrington, *The Poetic Edda*, p7). Notably, one of the villagers in the Doctor's makeshift army was at one point a one-eyed woman (TCH #81, p88).

[181] Snorri Sturluson, *Edda*, p13.

[182] Snorri Sturluson, *Edda*, p17; Lindow, *Norse Mythology*, pp231-232.

is worth noting Mímir's striking parallel with the decapitated heads of Dorium Maldovar and Handles, both of which served in previous Moffat-penned stories as quasi-oracles in imparting crucial, cryptic information to the Doctor[183]. Óðinn also obtains information from two ravens which perch on his shoulders, Huginn ('thought') and Muninn ('memory'), earning him the name Hrafnaguð ('raven-god')[184]. The bird, of course, looms large in *Face the Raven* (2015), there fulfilling its more traditional function as emblem of death and mortality, an association frequently made in skaldic poetry, and adding yet another Norse strand to Series 9's tapestry[185].

Ravens do not appear alongside 'Odin' in *The Girl Who Died* as broadcast, although Mathieson's fifth draft described the Mire leader as having a raven on either shoulder as part of his disguise, a detail that was ultimately cut[186]. Muninn is implicitly evoked, however, when the Doctor detects something unusual about Ashildr simply by looking at her, describing this strange premonition in typical time-traveller fashion as 'remembering [i.e., looking to the past] in the wrong direction'. Memory will turn out to be another recurring interest of this series of **Doctor Who**, from

---

[183] In *The Wedding of River Song* and *The Time of the Doctor* (2013). It should be noted that eyepatches also recur throughout Series 6, at one point even being worn by Gantok, a character wearing a Viking-inspired horned helmet; Wiggins argues in 'Odin and the Doctor' that Series 6 effectively retells the mythological story of the death of Baldr.

[184] Snorri Sturluson, *Edda*, p33.

[185] For further discussion of ravens see Groenewegen, Sarah, *The Black Archive #20: Face the Raven*. They are also a recurring motif in the TV series **Vikings** (2013-20) and in **Game of Thrones**.

[186] TCH #81, pp96, 99.

Colony Sarff's refrain that 'Davros knows. Davros remembers'[187] to the Zygons' ability to 'pluck loved ones from your memory and wear their faces'[188], from Ashildr's inability to retain details of her own life without writing them down to the memory-wipe ethical dilemma staged in *Hell Bent*.

According to John Berger, creator of the landmark television series (and accompanying book) *Ways of Seeing* (1972), 'our vision is continually active, continually moving, continually holding things in a circle around itself, constituting what is present to us as we are.'[189] He might almost have been describing *The Girl Who Died*'s final 'metaphorical sequence'[190], in which Bazalgette's camera circles around an unmoving Ashildr as the sun and stars rise and fall in the sky around her, a microcosm of the passing decades and centuries she will endure. She remains motionless in her spatial and temporal 'present' while space and time alike unfold and elapse in her line of view. Her newly acquired immortality means that, although she remains in one place staring straight ahead, her vision is 'continually moving' because her surroundings – the people and places she has known and loved – are subject to the entropic mercy of time's arrow.

---

[187] *The Magician's Apprentice*.

[188] *The Zygon Invasion*. Much like the Sontarans, the Zygons haunt the Mire: Mathieson conceived of their having 'old school Zygon sounding' voices (TCH #81, p95), notable given his own terror on first viewing *Terror of the Zygons* (1975) as a child (Arnopp, 'Immortal Words', DWM #493) and fitting well with the theme of perception versus reality. A Zygon story was also one of his initial pitches for Series 9 (TCH #81, p86).

[189] Berger, John, *Ways of Seeing*, p9.

[190] Cooper, *Steven Moffat's Doctor Who*, p158.

This bravura sequence, singled out for praise by critics[191], highlights the way *The Girl Who Died* deals not so much with 'Ways of Seeing', but rather 'Ways of Viewing'. Like many Moffat-era **Doctor Who** stories, it is fundamentally interested in asking what it **means** to be a **Doctor Who** story, especially a story told through the medium of television. Unlike other visual art forms, televisual media display images following one another as experienced in sequence, 'unfold[ing] in time'[192]. The centring of Ashildr's eyes in the frame, together with her changing facial expressions, draws attention to the way she is being altered by what she is viewing. The next chapter will explore the story's presentation of Ashildr in greater depth, but here it suffices to say that she is established as an Odinic character in the same vein as the Doctor in various respects, including the emphasis placed on her power of sight.

This theme is reinforced even in the seemingly generic one-off villains. As Tat Wood puts it, pointing to the Latin verb 'monstrare' (to show or to indicate), 'monsters [...] are there to be looked at'[193]. The Mire perform the most basic function of a monster in this etymological sense, in that they are de**monstr**ative: 'Odin' reveals himself as a vision of a gigantic divine head in the sky, while they ensure the villagers can hear the thunderous sound of their craft's 'weapon forges' as a display of performative strength meant to

---

[191] Cooper, *Steven Moffat's Doctor Who*, p158; Mulkern, Patrick, '**Doctor Who**: *The Girl Who Died*', *Radio Times*; Campbell, 'The Eyes Have It'.
[192] Berger, *Ways of Seeing*, p26.
[193] Wood, Tat, 'The Empire of the Senses: Narrative Form and Point-of-View in **Doctor Who**' in Butler, ed, *Time and Relative Dissertations in Space*, p96.

intimidate. This ability is in effect turned back on them, in that they are defeated through the manipulation of images: Ashildr's vivid imagination in tandem with the technological properties of a Mire helmet enhances her wooden puppet into a fully-fledged sea serpent or dragon[194]. The Mire are thus fooled (and indeed intimidated) by a performative illusion. 'Images,' writes Berger, 'were first made to conjure up the appearances of something that was absent'[195] – much as the Mire army's reputation is reliant on the story, the illusion, of their fearsome prowess, and much as the wooden puppet is an evocation of an absent monster.

This monster's appearance at the story's climax is also nothing more than an image, albeit a more sophisticated CGI one. Indeed, since it is the technology in the Mire's helmets which is projecting it, the CGI monster is, literally, a computer-generated image within the fiction itself. The upgrade from motionless puppet to moving televisual image momentarily obscures the fact that the object remains, in reality, a motionless puppet. In failing to perceive its true nature, the Mire warriors are tricked by an absence masquerading as a presence. They and their leader 'Odin' are undone by extremely Odinic weaponry – tricks, illusions, and the power of visual perception, illustrating yet again that the Doctor is

---

[194] The explicit connection with the Miðgarðsorm Jǫrmungandr, of Norse mythology (a huge serpent which coiled around the entire world), is made in TCH #81, p95. The presence of this image is reflective of another absence, in that at one point the story involved a real sea serpent being used by the Mire as a method of terror (TCH #81, p86).

[195] Berger, *Ways of Seeing*, p10. In the context of the Doctor and Óðinn as quasi-magicians, note Berger's use of the word 'conjure'.

far more akin to the mythological Óðinn than this posturing bully can hope to be. In targeting, and even altering, the Mire leader's way of viewing the world, the Doctor shows him the briefest glimpse of a far superior way.

This, then, is a story which not only aligns the Doctor with his most obvious counterpart in the Norse pantheon, but also deals explicitly with that deity's foremost trait: Óðinn's desire, and ability, to **see and understand things**. Comparing these two figures has revealed that, among other things, the Doctor and Óðinn share a hunger for knowledge that drives them to travel and explore. *The Girl Who Died* ties this knowledge to the power of sight and the ability to perform trickery and illusion, in keeping with what is known of the mythological Óðinn, and reiterates this throughout its runtime. It is important to bear in mind that this is also the story in which the Doctor realises – gains insight into – the reason why he is wearing his current face. In doing so, the comparison of 'real' and 'fake' faces points conclusively to the Doctor's fundamental role as Odinic healer.

3.3: 'Says the Man with a Fake Face'

The truths behind two faces are revealed over the course of *The Girl Who Died*, and unsurprisingly this, too, adds to the existing dichotomy between the Doctor and the Mire leader. The former experiences a moment of 'anagnorisis' – Aristotle's term for 'recognition'[196], referring to an instant in a story when a character realises something fundamental about their or another character's identity. In the Doctor's case, he realises what exactly his

[196] Aristotle, in Butcher, SH, trans, *The Poetics of Aristotle*, p41.

subconscious has been trying to tell him about the face he currently possesses. 'Odin' experiences no such moment of discovery but does nonetheless unveil the 'truth' of his own face in the story, unmasking his disguise to reveal the lamprey-like alien visage beneath. Yet again, protagonist and antagonist are juxtaposed in ways which illustrate fundamental differences, this time in the form of what these revelations about their 'real' faces say about them as characters.

Let us start with the more straightforward of the two. We only get a brief glimpse of his true face, but it is clear that the Mire leader 'Odin' resembles the rest of his species. In order to deceive the ninth-century Vikings whose testosterone he wishes to imbibe, he employs a 'convincing hologram' to disguise himself as the most powerful and prominent god in their pantheon. To achieve this, he draws on various clichéd tropes to present as archetypal an image of Odin as possible, from the eyepatch to the winged helmet (even, originally, including ravens in the ensemble).

However, 'Odin' bastardises the mythical Óðinn's identity, not because he poses as the god (so does the Doctor), but because he adopts a very specific, very narrow view of who Óðinn is, filtered through his own warmongering ideology. The physical appearance might match common depictions of the mythological Óðinn, but the hyper-masculine, testosterone-swigging deity he presents himself as is for the most part a distortion, a simplification – much as far-right extremists distort Norse symbols and iconography in the real world. Such distortions hide the fundamentally ugly truth which lies beneath, whether a lamprey from space or a set of noxious ideological beliefs, or – as in this case – both.

This is worlds apart from the Doctor's moment of anagnorisis regarding his own 'true' face. Having caught a glimpse of his own reflection, the Doctor recalls the questions he posed in the previous series' *Deep Breath* (2014): 'Who frowned me this face? Why this one? Why did I choose this face? [...] It's like I'm trying to tell myself something'. The present Doctor claims to have worked out what exactly he was 'trying to say' by choosing this face, prompting another flashback, this time to the events of *The Fires of Pompeii* (2008), which guest starred Peter Capaldi as marble tradesman Lobus Caecilius.

Therefore, the logic given here runs that, since the 10th Doctor made a deliberate choice to save Caecilius, his later incarnation's subconscious has settled on the same (albeit slightly older) facial features as a permanent reminder to himself to save people even in the direst circumstances. His identity becomes bound up in his face on a level beyond the literal: no longer simply an aspect of his appearance, it becomes an exhortation to behave in a certain way, a subconscious attempt 'to hold [himself] to the mark'. It is a 'fake face' of a different kind, almost a Platonic ideal – it has been borrowed from someone else but is now emblematic of a mantle he has taken on and must live up to. This certainly fits with Moffat's broader conception of the Doctor as an idealised identity he strives to uphold, which is on full display in Series 9[197].

---

[197] E.g., 'there's no such thing as the Doctor. I'm just a bloke in a box, telling stories... [but] sometimes, on a good day, if I try very hard, I'm not some old Time Lord who ran away. I'm the Doctor' (*The Witch's Familiar* (2015) and 'The Doctor is no longer here! You are stuck with me' (*Face the Raven*).

One could quite reasonably argue that this is a baffling creative decision that feels out of place in this particular story[198], or that audiences were not clamouring for and, moreover, did not **need** explanations for something as commonplace as an actor taking on different roles. Furthermore, this is surely even more superfluous in a long-running, cosmos-sprawling series like **Doctor Who**, which has over the years featured a host of recurring and guest actors giving performances in wildly different, completely unconnected parts, almost invariably without appended explanations[199].

Indeed, this aspect of the story came in for its fair share of criticism along these lines. One reviewer described 'the whiff of sphincters tightening' at this revelation as the story's only real 'lapse', adding that 'the fannish impulse to close a continuity loophole is best resisted'[200]. Another similarly felt that 'the fan service quotient is becoming dangerously high' and described the plot point as 'answering a question that no one needed an answer to in the first place'[201]. It could, certainly, be argued that calling back to a fairly specific detail of another episode broadcast seven and a half years earlier constitutes too great a leap for the more casual audience, or even for the proportion of regular viewers less prone to fannishly

---

[198] It is certainly true that it was a relatively late addition, appearing only in the seventh (read-through) draft and the shooting script itself (TCH #81, p99).

[199] Perhaps the most famous example prior to this point was sixth Doctor Colin Baker's turn as Commander Maxil in *Arc of Infinity* (1983), although another also occurs in *The Fires of Pompeii*, with Karen Gillan appearing as a soothsayer two years before the debut of Amy Pond.

[200] Mulkern, '*The Girl Who Died*'.

[201] Burk, in *Who Is the Doctor 2*, p184.

tightening sphincters.

On the other hand, this dramatic instance of facial (self-)recognition is perfectly in tune with what the rest of the story is doing, making it far from merely a shoehorned-in attempt to solve a continuity issue[202]. As has already been established, *The Girl Who Died* is interested in the ways in which the Doctor and 'Odin' succeed and fail at evoking the mythological Óðinn, and the attendant gulf between appearance and reality. Within this context, the Doctor's anagnorisis is essential to the episode and indeed to Series 9 as a whole. His recollection of his face's origin confirms for him that his 'true' identity is as a 'Doctor', a man who saves people by dancing around formalised rules – in short, as an Odinic trickster-healer. This is what is meant by soteriological trickery: cheating and deception with a moral force behind it, that fundamentally offers salvation. It is exactly the sort of thing practised by the man from the stars who used a time machine to cheat the rules and save a Pompeiian family from the fires of Vesuvius. This realisation alters not only the seemingly inevitable ending of *The Girl Who Died*, explicitly rejecting the fatalism inherent in the story's title, but it will also have wider – not entirely positive – ramifications for Ashildr, the Doctor and Clara throughout the rest of the 2015 run, culminating in the triptych of

---

[202] It is also not entirely without precedent in **Doctor Who**: *Destiny of the Daleks* (1979), *Smith and Jones* (2007) and *Journey's End* went to varying lengths to clarify the facial similarities between two characters played by the same performer. However, none of these applied to the series' lead, nor did the explanations given form the crux of a resolution to a problem or a major personal epiphany, as in this instance.

Face the Raven, *Heaven Sent*, and *Hell Bent*.

In a story which already draws significantly from mythology, it is noteworthy that the flashback sequence designed to 'explain' the origin of the Doctor's face codifies **Doctor Who** itself as myth – one offering salvation at the hands of a demigod. There is the same sense of an echo of an ancient story coming to bear upon the material reality of the present. Its relative antiquity is amplified further by the fact that many children watching would not have been born when *The Fires of Pompeii* was broadcast, or would at least have had no memory of it. Tellingly, *Pompeii* is also a story in which the programme itself is mythic – literally so, in that the Doctor and Donna become the Caecilius family's 'household gods'. Moreover, this particular face – and, fittingly, these particular eyes – have already taken on greater iconic emphasis than usual in their sudden, unexpected, but rapturously received cameo appearance in the 50th anniversary special, *The Day of the Doctor* (2013), a pivotal moment in the programme's own mythos.

Much as the trappings of Norse mythology underpin Ashildr's arc across the rest of the series, so too is this aspect of **Doctor Who** mythology configured here as the focus of a sentimental, even melodramatic, catharsis. In this respect, *The Girl Who Died* reflects what Matthew Hills has observed about modern **Doctor Who**'s use of mythology. Rather than adhering to the template adopted by structural anthropologists such as Claude Lévi-Strauss, in which mythology constitutes a system of known symbols arranged to form meaning, Hills recognises this approach as fundamentally rooted in 'internal character emotion-states' and the way they shape and blur with 'external narrative realities'[203].

Mythology – all mythology, Norse and **Who** alike – matters to us and holds sway over us not simply because it is old or venerable or part of a grand tradition, nor simply because of an interplay of symbols, but because of how it makes the relevant characters feel and act, and by extension how it affects our own emotional states. This is exactly what happens here: the actions of the 12th Doctor's former self directly prompt a revelation of great personal importance ('I'm the Doctor, and I save people!') and an act born of kindness and compassion, but which will have huge emotional consequences for all involved. Used well, mythology does not detract from the drama; it enriches it.

This dramatic, mythic anagnorisis is precipitated by the Doctor seeing his own reflection in the surface of a barrel of water – echoing his contemplation of his new face in a mirror in his first story, *Deep Breath*, a brief clip from which also appears in flashback. This instant of self-recognition evokes psychoanalyst Jacques Lacan's 'mirror stage', in which infants come to recognise their own image in a mirror or other reflective surface and for the first time perceive themselves as an external object outside of their own subjective existence. According to Lacan, this moment of 'identification' offers infant minds the possibility of resolving this apparent contradiction into a unified whole over which they possess full control. This 'Aha-Erlebnis' ('Aha-experience') is a kind

---

[203] Hills, Matthew, '"Mythology Makes You Feel Something": The Russell T Davies Era as Sentimental Journey", in Burdge, Anthony, Jessica Burke, and Kristine Larsen, eds, *The Mythological Dimensions of Doctor Who*, p208.

of epiphany or anagnorisis not unlike the Doctor's[204].

He may have wanted to see a children's menu, but the 12th Doctor is not, in fact, a child[205]. Yet something of the same 'mirror stage' effect is at work here. The unique circumstances of regeneration mean that a single subjective identity occupies multiple successive external existences and must re-identify with each in turn. Thus, any one case of the Doctor grappling with their new identity – especially in a post-regeneration story such as *Deep Breath*, in which they are effectively a new-born – finds an intriguing parallel in the infant struggling to piece together its 'fragmented body'[206].

This is yet another area in which the Doctor and Óðinn resemble one another, in that the Norse god has a similarly mercurial physical form; Snorri tells us that 'Óðinn changed shapes', would lay down as if 'asleep or dead' and become 'a bird or an animal, a fish or a snake'[207]. Their status as transgressive Tricksters applies not just to behaviour or capricious whim, but even to such apparent certainties as physical appearance and species. For this reason, the Doctor's moment of identification feeds directly into not only his alignment with the mythological Óðinn but also the episode's prominent theme of interrogating external realities.

---

[204] Lacan, Jacques, 'The Mirror Stage as Formative of the *I* Function as Revealed in Psychoanalytic Experience', in Fink, Bruce, trans, *Écrits*, pp75-76.
[205] *Deep Breath*.
[206] Lacan, 'The Mirror Stage', p78.
[207] Snorri Sturluson, *Heimskringla Vol 1*, p10. It has been suggested in the past that the Doctor and other Time Lords can change species after death – see *Doctor Who* (1996) and, for a slightly different demonstration, *Destiny of the Daleks*.

The Girl Who Died presents us with a Doctor who finally **sees** a fundamental truth about his own identity in its simplest form, a truth bound up in his face as material reminder of his mythic emotional history. He recalls that he is the Doctor, and that he saves people; he beats the Mire at their own game of performative illusions and uses the sci-fi equivalent of sorcery to bring a girl back from the dead. Nowhere else is the Doctor's position as a latter-day Óðinn more explicit: comfortable playing the role of trickster, but also embracing the legacy of healer.

CHAPTER 4: THE HYBRID WARRIOR-WOMAN

While the eponymous character in *The Girl in the Fireplace* (2006) was a one-off guest star and love interest, and *The Girl Who Waited* (2011) refers to a frequent nickname for the Doctor's then-companion, the 'Girl Who Died' is something halfway between the two. Ashildr initially seems little more than a guest star of the week, but is soon promoted to the more significant role of recurring character, appearing in another three episodes of Series 9. This chapter examines this complex figure and the way in which she echoes transgressive warrior-women of Viking history and mythology, through the etymology of her name, her ascension towards immortality, and her genderqueer identity. Additionally, the story's queer and feminising subtext will be weighed up against its general dearth of female characters other than Clara and Ashildr – whilst pointing out the additional girl at the heart of the episode who tends to be overlooked.

4.1: 'In a Way… She's a Hybrid'

A previous **Black Archive** volume has already identified Ashildr's name as meaning 'battle of the gods'[208]. 'Hildr', or 'battle', appears as a constituent part in the names of various women from Old

---

[208] Groenewegen, *Face the Raven*, p37. Another possible source for the name is a conflation of Álfhildr and Ása, two successive queens of the same Vestfold king (Snorri Sturluson, *Heimskringla Vol 1*, p45) and both plausible candidates for the high-status woman honoured in the Oseberg ship burial chamber (Jesch, Judith, *Women in the Viking Age*, p34).

Norse-Icelandic sources, such as Brynhildr, and is also a given name for a particular Valkyrie, often portrayed in skaldic verse as the literal embodiment of battle itself[209]. The first part of Ashildr's name is closer to the Old Norse 'áss' or 'ás', a singular god, than it is to either the definite genitive plural 'of the gods' ('ásanna') or the indefinite genitive plural 'of gods' ('ása'). The literal translation of 'Ashildr' would therefore be 'god-battle' but, since the second noun modifies the first, 'battle of god/gods' is probably the best translation; this could also be rendered as 'divine battle'. *The Girl Who Died* does, as we have seen, contain a conflict between two competing versions of 'Odin', while the Doctor will (briefly) clash with another quasi-deity, 'Rassilon the redeemer'[210], in a later episode in which Ashildr appears. It seems slightly strange to name a prominent female guest star after conflicts between male figures, however, even if you can make the argument that the Doctor and 'Odin' are fighting over her (as personification of the village as a whole). Another route is to decouple the two nouns from the compound and simply focus on them as key elements of Ashildr's character and the extent to which she is associated with both warfare and divinity. The name therefore suitably emphasises her status throughout Series 9 as both a warrior and an immortal being, and foregrounds key elements of her agency and personality.

The two components of Ashildr's name refer to two essential parts of her nature throughout her character arc: her belligerent spirit

---

[209] Snorri Sturluson, *Edda*, p31; *Grimnismál* stanza 36 (Larrington, *The Poetic Edda*, p53). It is also the name of a nun/warrior-woman in **The Last Kingdom**.
[210] *Hell Bent*.

and aptitude in battle, and her immortality. The name is fitting to the point of being an aptronym (a name matching its bearer's character or occupation). Her immortality is prominently conferred on her at the end of the story, but her warlike nature is showcased throughout: she thinks in terms of strategy ('swords against these creatures. That won't work, will it?'); using a wooden stave, she play-acts at duelling with a puppet version of 'Fake Odin'; and, perhaps most memorably, it is her act of challenging the Mire and statement that 'We will crush you on the field of battle' that leads to war between them and the villagers. This warlike side of Ashildr resurfaces in *The Woman Who Lived*: she regularly wields pistols and recounts that she served in the Hundred Years' War, during which – she boasts – she could 'shoot six arrows a minute' and 'got so close to the enemy [she] penetrated armour'[211].

While it would be incorrect to declare warriorhood and immortality incompatible, there is something nonetheless hybrid-like about an immortal warrior. Warriors, both in general and in Old Norse-Icelandic literature in particular, are frequently defined by their role in battle, the omnipresent risk of death, and the valour and bravery involved in facing it. Immortals generally transcend this risk. It takes a special set of circumstances for Norse warriors to be immortalised – they must first be killed, selected from the battlefields by the Valkyries ('valkyrjur' or 'choosers of the slain'), resurrected, and brought to live in Valhǫll where they are free to fight eternally[212]. What happens to Ashildr at the end of *The Girl*

[211] *The Woman Who Lived.* Additionally, in early drafts of *Girl*, Ashildr was explicitly trained as a warrior alongside the men of the village (TCH #81, p91).
[212] See e.g., Snorri Sturluson, *Edda*, pp31-4; and *Vafþrúðnismál*,

Who Died evokes a fairly common Norse motif: she is a warrior who is resurrected by a higher power and made immortal.

Ashildr's ascension to the position of 'immortal warrior' is very much in keeping with the broader concerns of the 2015 run of episodes. Indeed, it makes for a fascinating parallel with what happens to Clara toward the end of the season. She, too, is effectively resurrected from certain death (in a typically cheeky **Doctor Who**ish flaunting of the usual chronology of 'resurrection', she is narratively brought back from death a second earlier, temporally speaking, than the moment of dying itself, even though the fact of her death remains intact). She, too, ascends towards a position of Doctorhood and quasi-divinity. It is fitting, then, that these two characters end up transcending the limitations of their roles within the programme by flying off(-screen) together and on to their own, undocumented adventures[213].

Even before Ashildr's resurrection and immortality, by which point she becomes a quasi-deity toying with others, there is a suggestion that she believes she can ensure her kin come home safe from raids and battles through 'mak[ing] up the right story'. This echoes

---

stanza 41 (Larrington, *The Poetic Edda*, p43).

[213] At least one **Doctor Who** writer views Clara and Ashildr's immortality through a distinctly Norse lens – see Wilkinson, Joy, *Doctor Who: The Witchfinders*, p178, where the pair, together with Willa Twiston, are referred to as both 'three girls from the North' and 'norns', the Norse equivalent of the Greek and Roman 'Fates'. Given what happens to Ashildr in *The Girl Who Died* and her potentially conferring immortality on Sam Swift in *The Woman Who Lived*, there is something fitting in her ending up with the cosmic role of determining the lifespans of others.

the role played by Valkyries in guarding or safekeeping favoured warriors, or the 'wood-maidens' referred to by Saxo Grammaticus whose 'guidance and government [...] mainly determined the fortunes of war [...] and [whose] secret assistance won for their friends the coveted victories'[214].

Toward the end of the series, however, Ashildr bargains with other people's lives and deaths in *Face the Raven* through the use of a quantum shade – dealing out death first to a denizen of Trap Street, and later to Clara (via Rigsy). While waiting out the end of the universe in *Hell Bent*, sitting in the ruins of Gallifrey's cloisters and sustaining her own 'reality bubble at the end of Time itself', she is explicitly depicted with a chess board in front of her[215]. **Doctor Who** fans might immediately think of the game's connection with the quasi-deity Fenric in a story full of Norse symbolism, and it is not inconceivable that the prop was intended as a cheeky hint to such fans that this entity might appear – as the mythical Hybrid, perhaps. In Norse mythology itself, however, there is another analogue in the form of the chess- or chequers-like pieces played with by the Æsir in the 10th-century poem *Vǫluspá*[216]. Rather than being a regular chess set, the pieces in

---

[214] Grammaticus, *Danish History*, p178.

[215] *Hell Bent.* The board is presumably an addition at the set design stage: its presence is not specified in the shooting script (Moffat, Steven, 'Hell Bent').

[216] *Vǫluspá*, stanzas 8 and 58 (Larrington, *The Poetic Edda*, pp5, 11). Although Larrington's translation offers 'chequers' as a familiar equivalent, the Norse board game (hnefa)tafl referred to in the poem was not identical to either modern chess or chequers. There is evidence that women of the Viking age played board games such as chess – see Jochens, Jenny, *Women in Old Norse Society*, p104.

front of Ashildr are all birds of various kinds – owls, eagles, parrots, and so on, 'rhyming' with the bird motif visible on her dress in the same scene. It is hard not to see these design choices as reiterating the role she played in Clara's fall at the hands of the quantum shade 'raven' – billions of years ago for her, but a mere two weeks for the viewer (on live broadcast at least). We are invited to wonder how many others have been forced to face the raven because of her, how many others' lives she has played with like pieces on a chessboard. She is a pawn who has become a queen.

Ashildr resembles one other immortal in Norse mythology: the mysteriously obscure figure of Gullveig, who may also be known as Heiðr and who in the whole Norse canon is only referred to in two stanzas of *Vǫluspá*[217]. Much like Ashildr, she is brought back to life when killed – although in her case on three occasions rather than one[218] – and in both cases, the deaths and resurrections take place in a hall against the backdrop (either as trigger or climax) of a larger conflict. Scholars have offered countless conflicting interpretations of who exactly Gullveig is (a giantess; a god; a sorceress)[219], rather aptly evoking a hybrid that defies easy categorisation. The 'gull' ('gold') part of her name might suggest she is in some way a personification of the corrupting influence of wealth, but, on the basis of 'veig' ('drink'), intoxication of a different kind has also been

[217] *Vǫluspá*, stanzas 22-23 (Larrington, *The Poetic Edda*, p6).

[218] Which does resemble Clara's 'three deaths', in *Asylum of the Daleks, The Snowmen* (2012), and *Face the Raven*.

[219] Kuusela, Tommy, 'Halls, Gods and Giants: The Enigma of Gullveig in Óðinn's Hall', in Wikström af Edholm, Klas et al, eds, *Myth, Materiality and Lived Religion: In Merovingian and Viking Scandinavia*, pp27-31.

suggested: mead, which is after all a golden drink[220]. This is not quite as bizarre an idea as it sounds, given the Norse origin myth of 'the mead of poetry', in which the ability to fashion great literature comes from, and is embodied in, ale[221].

In other words, following the associative symbolic logic of Norse poetry, a personification of mead could be read as a personification of storytelling itself – not at all dissimilar to the role played by Ashildr, who is explicitly described as a 'storyteller' in this episode and has an entire library's worth of stories from her own life in the next. We will return to this idea, but the intriguing parallels with Gullveig only enhance the sense of Ashildr as a unique, distinctive figure set apart from the rest of her society – othered through her new-found immortality by the end of the story, most obviously, but also as a storyteller in a culture (Norse) and a universe (that in which **Who** takes place) where stories have almost supernatural power.

Finally, Ashildr is also a hybrid between one-off character and regular cast member, in a way that plays with audience expectations. The initial announcement that Maisie Williams, star of **Game of Thrones**, would appear in Series 9 did not intimate that she would be anything more than a guest character in a single adventure[222]. Williams' high profile, the string of awards to her

---

[220] Höckert, Robert, *Vǫluspá och vanakulten*, pp116-117; Motz, Lotte, 'Gullveig's Ordeal. A New Interpretation', in *Arkiv för nordisk filologi* 108, pp82-85.

[221] Snorri Sturluson, *Edda*, pp61-64.

[222] BBC Media Centre, 'Doctor Who Reveals Maisie Williams as Guest Star'.

name, and the salary she could presumably command might have meant many viewers were surprised that **Doctor Who** managed to attract her to a recurring role rather than a mere guest spot. Contrary to what one might expect, the part was **not** specifically written for her. Ashildr was scripted originally as an older, married woman but had been refashioned as both younger and more warlike before casting began, while Williams' performance as Arya Stark was less of a deciding factor in Brian Minchin's choice to approach her than her lead role in *Cyberbully* (2015)[223]. However, the series paratext – external material outside the 'text' of the episodes themselves, such as marketing, previews, and trailers – clearly focussed on Williams' **Game of Thrones** fame, the most notable example being the *Radio Times* cover for the week of broadcast[224].

Both within the narrative and in the real world, then, Ashildr is something of a hybrid. The Doctor's comment to that effect at the end of *The Girl Who Died* refers to the fact that she is now an immortal with 'a little piece of alien inside her'. Even before that transformation, however, there is something hybridic or transgressive about her identity, specifically in the extent to which she has a genderqueer identity. In addition to her warrior-like

---

[223] TCH #81, pp88-95, 97.

[224] The cover bears the heading '**Doctor Who** Meets **Game of Thrones**!' with a prominent picture of Capaldi, Coleman, and Williams (*Radio Times*, 17 October 2015). The subheading 'But will Maisie Williams be the new companion?', makes clear that by this point Ashildr was being marketed not only as a significant series character but even – if only as unofficial suggestion – as a replacement for the imminently departing Coleman.

nature, this aspect echoes the way transgressive women warriors are presented in Norse mythology and what we know of Viking society.

4.2: 'Everyone Knows I'm Strange. But Here I'm Loved.'

In the form of Ashildr, *The Girl Who Died* largely plays into the 'widespread view that women in the Viking age were forceful, independent and powerful'[225]. Various 13th-century sagas depict Norse women of earlier periods as 'strong and vengeful'[226], but elsewhere there is the even more memorable trope of women as fully-fledged warriors. This persistent motif can be found in a variety of sources, including the Oserberg tapestry, on which women are depicted with spears; Snorri's *Edda*, which depicts the formidable Skaði, 'odd-woman out among the goddesses', as bearing 'helmet and mail-coat and all weapons of war'; the heroic poem *Atlakviða*, in which Guðrún exacts bloody revenge, adopting 'a male prerogative'; Saxo Grammaticus' 12th-century *Gesta Danorum*, which grumbles with disapproval about heathen women who dared to be warriors or pirates; the Byzantine historian John Skylitzes' account of finding the corpses of armoured women among the Rus' (Norse settlers in eastern Europe); and the aforementioned Valkyries found in skaldic poetry and other mythological sources[227].

---

[225] Jesch, *Women in the Viking Age*, p4.
[226] Jesch, *Women in the Viking Age*, p114.
[227] Jesch, *Women in the Viking Age*, pp124, 139, 147; Snorri Sturluson, *Edda*, p61; Grammaticus, *Danish History*, p431; Skylitzes, John, in Wortley, John, trans, *A Synopsis of Byzantine History 811-*

There is also some archaeological evidence to support the idea, most notably in the form of the bodies of women who were buried with weapons. While axes and knives could be dismissed as nothing more than kitchen implements, the identification of the individual in Bj 581, a warrior grave in Sweden, as 'a high ranking female Viking warrior' complete with sword, shields, and 'armour-piercing arrows', suggests that 'women, indeed, were able to be full members of male dominated spheres'[228]. Although this particular find postdates the episode, it is an example of the phenomenon Mathieson is referring to when he mentions researching 'Viking women buried with [...] swords'[229].

To an extent, the accuracy of such depictions is largely beside the point; in relying on even a fictitious or exaggerated conception of warrior women, *The Girl Who Died* follows in a long tradition inherited not just from saga literature but also various pop culture depictions of Vikings. The earliest example of a woman in film or television dressing up as a Viking warrior is probably Helga in the 1928 film *The Viking*. More recent Norse (or Norse-adjacent) warrior-women characters include (perhaps most obviously) Williams' Arya in **Game of Thrones**, as well as Brienne of Tarth; Éowyn in *The Lord of the Rings* and its film adaptations; Brida, Hild, Aethelflaed, and Stiorra in **The Last Kingdom**; Lagertha, Astrid, Gunnhild, and Þórunn in **Vikings** (although that programme's notion of an entire legion of shieldmaidens is almost certainly

---

1057, p290.

[228] Hedenstierna-Jonson, Charlotte et al, 'A Female Viking Warrior Confirmed by Genetics', in *American Journal of Physical Anthropology* 164:4, p858.

[229] TCH #81, p91.

exaggerated); Frøya in **Norsemen**; and Sif, Hela, and Valkyrie (all based on mythological figures) in Marvel's **Thor** comics and films, not to mention Jane Foster's ascension to her 'Mighty Thor' persona.

Such characters tend to walk a line somewhere between empowered and objectified, depending on how they are written, filmed, and (particularly) dressed – a manifestation of one of the paradoxes of mainstream Western culture of the 21st century, that violent displays of female emancipation must be tempered by an (un)healthy degree of titillation in the mix for the fantasies of the male audience. As one medieval historian put it, 'the idea of warrior women performs the distinctive feat of appealing simultaneously to heterosexual male fantasies of liberated Amazons and to feminist aspirations of finding powerful women in past societies'[230].

A similarly ambiguous depiction can be found in Old Norse-Icelandic sources. On the one hand, such female warriors 'were frequently admired for qualities normally associated with men', through positive descriptors such as 'drengr' (valiant) or 'skǫrungr' (forceful)[231]. Women who donned armour or exacted bloody

---

[230] Trafford, 'Hyper-Masculinity vs Viking Warrior-Women'. See, for example, the snappily-titled film *The Saga of the Viking Women and their Voyage to the Waters of the Great Sea Serpent* (1958), in which Viking women in impractically short skirts do indeed have an adventure of their own and free their menfolk from captivity – but are only motivated to set off in the first place by their pining for the men in question, and of course it is a man who ultimately dispatches the sea serpent.

[231] Jochens, *Women in Old Norse Society*, p61.

revenge were presented as praiseworthy in the eyes of some saga authors or poets because they had assumed supposedly masculine characteristics – Auðr, for example, in *Íslendingabók* and *Laxdæla Saga*, who 'clearly commanded respect', or *Atlakviða*'s Gudrún, who is praised as a 'bright woman'[232]. In 1993, Carol Clover suggested that Norse gender roles be best understood not so much in terms of a simplistic male/female binary but a flexible (yet undoubtedly still misogynist) spectrum ranging from 'hvatr' (virile/strong) to 'blauðr' (feminine/weak). The idea behind this spectrum was that any individual, regardless of sex, could move along it throughout life depending on their behaviour – with it being clearly desirable to stay hvatr (in the domain of the masculine warrior) and avoid slipping into being blauðr (the domestic sphere of women, children, and older, infirm, or more effeminate men)[233]. This echoes the principle of 'hegemonic masculinity': a hierarchy of gendered behaviour, with a dominant form of masculinity at the top and 'feebler' or more feminine masculinity ranked toward the bottom. By and large, then, in the Norse sphere at least, it was the (conventionally) masculine rather than the feminine which was 'the human ideal that was most

---

[232] Jesch, *Women in the Viking Age*, p83; *Atlakviða*, stanza 43 (Larrington, *The Poetic Edda*, p210).

[233] Clover, Carol J, 'Regardless of Sex: Men, Women and Power in Early Northern Europe', *Speculum* 68:2, pp363-87. Clover's spectrum has been criticised (e.g., by Jóhanna Katrín Friðriksdóttir) for being too simplistic, however, in presuming that masculine behaviour was the principal route by which Norse women achieved power and status.

admired and to which both men and women aspired'[234].

On the other hand, multiple texts harshly criticise warrior-women for their transgression in aspiring towards masculine attributes. Christian authors such as Saxo Grammaticus typically depict them as being ultimately defeated as a direct result of their supposedly disgraceful pagan behaviour[235]. Various sagas depict women as vengeful inciters, criticising them for 'represent[ing] the bad old days, the heathen past' because they carry weapons or don men's clothing; it has been argued that such women 'were a useful and colourful myth that accounted for the horrors of violence while removing the blame for it from male shoulders'[236]. Similarly, the male-presenting Maiden-Kings, who appear in the Icelandic rímur poems and with whom Ashildr has several traits in common, invariably end up defeated, humiliated, and subjected to the whims of their male suitors so that the balance of gender roles can be properly restored. In many ways this is not surprising: '[the Maiden-Kings'] rogue masculinity,' as one critic puts it, 'threaten[ed] to upset the patriarchal order itself', betraying a 'latent anxiety in Norse culture about female aggression rising up in response to masculine deficiencies amongst men'[237]. Lastly, the medieval Icelandic laws known as *Grágás* explicitly forbade cross-

---

[234] Jochens, *Women in Old Norse Society*, p162.
[235] Jesch, *Women in the Viking Age*, pp177-78.
[236] Jesch, *Women in the Viking Age*, pp185, 191.
[237] Layher, William, 'Caught Between Worlds: Gendering the Maiden Warrior in Old Norse', in Poor, Sara S, and Jana K Schulman, eds, *Women and Medieval Epic: Gender, Genre and the Limits of Epic Masculinity*, p202.

dressing 'for the sake of being different'[238]. It is important not to misleadingly overstate the gender politics of the Viking Age as being somehow profoundly progressive havens of tolerant fluidity, however attractive such revisionism might be.

It is difficult to determine or identify Ashildr's gender identity for multiple reasons. She is played by a cisgender female actor and almost always uses feminine pronouns, while the episode titles refer to her as 'Girl' and 'Woman'; but she is masculine-coded within the text in several ways. She is a fictional character within a historical (or quasi-historical) setting that is far removed from our contemporary understanding of, and language around, gender. At the same time, however, she is a character written in the 2010s, who thus does exist within the context of contemporary queer terminology. Certainly, there is no evidence – either textual or extratextual – that the character as written was intended as explicit representation of a trans man, and so the writers should not receive praise for making that deliberate choice. Nonetheless, in various ways she maps onto a historical-cultural archetype (a broad umbrella including butch women) which has been meaningfully appreciated by or related to by trans men, and the extent to which such viewers could identify with the character should be acknowledged.

On balance the weight of evidence probably leans towards reading her as genderqueer or non-binary in some capacity, i.e., somewhere between the twin poles of male and female. The strongest piece of evidence is her declaration, in one of the episode's most moving passages, that:

---

[238] Layher, 'Caught Between Worlds', p186.

> 'I've always been different. All my life I've known that. The girls all thought I was a boy. The boys all said I was just a girl. My head is always full of stories. I know I'm strange. Everyone knows I'm strange. But here I'm loved'.

These sentiments have been particularly praised for their depiction of a child 'who didn't fit in with the girls or the boys [...] but **was loved anyway**'[239]. Some might argue this is a romanticised or idealistic view of how openly medieval Scandinavian society might have welcomed either a non-binary individual or transgressive warrior-woman. As has already been established, however, excessive fidelity to modern-day anthropological understanding of Viking culture is not high on *The Girl Who Died*'s agenda. Instead, it seems to be a priority of the above passage to assure viewers – especially children or teenagers who do not fit in with gendered societal expectations about what it means to behave like a boy or a girl, whether because they are queer or non-binary, or simply because of their interests – that there is nothing wrong with being different from a socially constructed 'norm', and that society can and should accept you for who you are[240]. Given the programme has a sizeable target audience who are young and impressionable,

---

[239] Rayner, Jacqueline, 'Relative Dimensions: Girl, Resurrected', DWM #493 (emphasis in original).

[240] This is reinforced in *The Woman Who Lived* by Ashildr accepting her identity as 'no one's mother, daughter, wife. My own companion,' furthering the queer subtext by rejecting the familiar structures of compulsory heteronormativity. She does not comment here on her sexuality, but clearly does not define herself in terms of standard 17th-century norms regarding marriage and reproduction.

delivering such a message is an unambiguous social good.

There **are** examples of genderqueer characters in Old Norse-Icelandic texts with whom Ashildr has certain traits in common, some more overtly supernatural than others. As Lee Colwill has phrased it in their recent discussion on the topic, certain texts express a conception of gender that is 'fundamentally defined through social perception and interaction'[241]. The aforementioned Maiden-Kings ('meykongr') are presented in the rímur and in subsequent sagas as women who ruled as male-presenting kings and insisted on being referred to with masculine pronouns, reacting with fury if this was not followed. Two especially prominent examples can be found in *Hervarar Saga ok Heiðreks* and *Hrólfs Saga Gautrekssonar,* where the women Hervǫr and Þornbjǫrg become the male warriors Hjǫrvarðr and Þórbergr, and the latter quite happily lives as male even when no one else is around, suggesting that this aspect of their identity is more than just a disguise[242]. Elsewhere, the elf-queen in the folkloric poem *Snjáskvæði* undergoes a 'gendered transformation'[243] into a human king; a breast-feeding male Viking appears in *Flóamanna saga*[244]; and a character in full body armour in both *Sigrdrífumál* and *Vǫlsunga saga* is referred to using masculine pronouns until their

---

[241] Colwill, Lee, 'The King's Two Bodies? *Snjáskvæði* and the Performance of Gender', p1.

[242] See Layher, 'Caught Between Worlds'; Colwill, 'The King's Two Bodies?', p60.

[243] Colwill, 'The King's Two Bodies?', p1.

[244] Guðbrandur Vigfússon, *Origines Islandicae: A Collection of the More Important Sagas and Other Native Writings Relating to the Settlement and Early History of Iceland*, Vol II, p649.

helmet is lifted to reveal that they are a woman underneath[245]. Additionally, there are several instances of genderfluidity among the pantheon of Norse gods: Loki turns into a mare, is impregnated by a stallion, and later gives birth; Þórr dresses as a bride to infiltrate the giants; and Óðinn is strongly linked to the magical art of 'seiðr', with all the associations of effeminacy and homosexuality that that implied[246].

One common factor across many of these examples is a focus on the external trappings of gender, e.g., masculine-coded clothing such as helmets and armour. Saxo Grammaticus refers to women who, in dressing as male warriors, 'unsexed themselves' or, in effect, 'took off' their womanhood[247]. It might seem odd to modern readers, in a world where hormone replacement therapy and sex reassignment surgery are possibilities, that male or female identity could be so decisively assumed purely on the basis of one's clothes. But it is worth remembering medieval Scandinavia's cold, many-layered climate and relative poverty, both of which led to minimal variety in everyday clothing and thus to individuals' identities being very much associated with what they wore[248]. In recognition of this, an early draft of *The Girl Who Died* involved Vikings mistaking

---

[245] *Sigrdrífumál*, prose introduction (Larrington, *The Poetic Edda*, p162); Finch, RG, ed and trans, *Vǫlsunga saga: The Saga of the Volsungs*, p35.

[246] On Loki, see Snorri Sturluson, *Edda*, p36; on Þórr, see *Thrymskviða* (Larrington, *The Poetic Edda*, pp93-7).

[247] Grammaticus, *Danish History*, p431.

[248] Colwill, 'The King's Two Bodies?', p52; Jochens, Jenny, 'Before the Male Gaze: The Absence of the Female Body in Old Norse', in Salisbury, Joyce E, ed, *Sex in the Middle Ages: A Book of Essays*, pp3-29.

'the Doctor's new companion' (as she was then) for a man purely because she was wearing trousers[249].

By contrast, Ashildr **is** explicitly dressed in tattered trousers rather than traditional women's clothing; since this fact goes unmentioned, it seems likely this is her regular attire[250]. Significantly, her death comes about as a result of her donning a masculine-coded object, an extremely bulky and unwieldy Mire helmet that is several sizes too large for her. At first glance, this is an echo of the way in which the Maiden-Kings are typically thwarted in their adoption of masculine attributes, but this rather cruel fate is not the end of her story: she progresses beyond the limitations which literary templates have previously imposed on genderqueer Norse figures. In *The Woman Who Lived*, she appears (in flashback) in medieval armour, as well as adopting the guise (and distinctly masculine voice, courtesy of a male actor) of a 17th-century highwayman, 'the Knightmare'. While in this disguise, she briefly adopts masculine pronouns. Her ascension toward the lordly or authoritative roles she plays on television such as a medieval queen, Lady Me, or Mayor Me, is another point in common with the Maiden-Kings.

Despite her status as a warrior that is resurrected and immortalised

---

[249] TCH #81, p89. To give an idea of how transgressive this would have been seen as, a character in *Laxdæla Saga* divorces his wife purely because she has been wearing men's breeches (trans Keneva Kunz, in Örnólfur Thorsson, ed, *The Sagas of Icelanders*, pp333-34).

[250] Early drafts also had her performing jobs that were traditionally masculine-coded in Norse society, such as armourer and carpenter (TCH #81, pp88, 94).

(typically the province of human soldiers resurrected by Valkyries), there are grounds for viewing Ashildr as Valkyrie-like herself: her belief that she can safeguard her village's warriors and bring them safely home, her acquiring the power of doling out death or resurrection to others (in the form of the second Mire repair kit, the quantum shade, and the suggestion in the novelisation of *The Witchfinders* (2018) that she goes on to determine the length of others' lifespans), and her association with a raven, commonly depicted as harbingers of death alongside Valkyries[251]. The critic Kathleen M Self has suggested that Valkyries formed a 'third gender' in the Norse understanding, one taking the form of 'a hybrid of masculine and feminine attributes'[252]; her choice of the word 'hybrid' naturally echoes Ashildr. This 'hybridity' manifests in Valkyries' possessing both masculine trappings (such as armour and weaponry) alongside feminine linguistic and literary markers (such as pronouns or poetic descriptors). The use of the word 'hybrid', with its implication that the result is an abnormal blend of two normal templates, to describe a real-world gender identity is quite tasteless and courts risk of both othering and stigmatisation. Nonetheless, its use in this context captures something of how genderqueer identities could have been seen in the Norse sphere as fundamentally transgressive, as something 'out of the ordinary'.

This transgressive quality knits together almost all the examples

---

[251] See e.g., *Hrafnsmál*, a poem that consists entirely of a conversation between a Valkyrie and a raven (Hollander, Lee M, ed and trans, *Old Norse Poems*, pp56-62).

[252] Self, Kathleen M, 'The Valkyrie's Gender: Old Norse Shield-Maidens and Valkyries as a Third Gender', *Feminist Formations* 26:1, p144.

discussed in this chapter – viewed by some historical sources with suspicion and unease, but clearly presented in the form of Ashildr as worthy of love and respect. The previous chapter paralleled the Doctor and Óðinn as a pair of transgressive Trickster figures, effectively magicians. It is worth dwelling for a moment on the connection between magic and queerness as related expressions of nonconforming. Witchcraft, known as 'seiðr', was explicitly viewed in Norse culture and mythology as a 'feminine' art practised by witches, something largely seen as emasculating for males to perform; to do so could lead to accusations of 'ergi', sexual perversion, the intended meaning of which was generally effeminacy or homosexuality[253]. Yet somehow, perhaps due to his unique status as sovereign deity, Óðinn is 'the only male figure who practises seiðr and gets away with it'[254]. One of the abilities seiðr allegedly granted was to 'predict the fates of men and things that had not yet happened', which is certainly rather Doctorish[255]. That the Doctor and Óðinn both have a certain affinity with the magical, therefore, resonates with queer readings of both outsider Trickster figures: each character 'exemplifies narratives of difference not sameness'[256].

---

[253] Loki accuses Óðinn of exactly this in *Lokasenna* stanza 24 (Larrington, *The Poetic Edda*, p85).

[254] Ármann Jakobsson, 'The Trollish Acts of Þorgrímr the Witch: The Meanings of *Troll* and *Ergi* in Medieval Iceland', *Saga-Book* XXXII, p58.

[255] Snorri Sturluson, *Heimskringla Vol 1*, p11. See, e.g., the little hints the Doctor is able to drop about individuals' futures in *Doctor Who* (1996).

[256] Solli, 'Queering the Cosmology of the Vikings', p194.

Ashildr is not a magician or sorceress as such. However, her resemblance to the mythical figure of Gullveig has already been noted; if Gullveig is understood as one and the same as the sorceress Heiðr ('the seer with pleasing prophecies' who 'practised spirit-magic'[257]), certain echoes come into sharper focus. *The Woman Who Lived* establishes that Ashildr has been ducked for being a witch after performing a healing miracle[258], while her use of the quantum shade 'raven', complete with eerie supernatural tattoo, bears the visual hallmarks of – and effectively obeys the rules of – magic. This motif would have been still more prominent in Mathieson's fourth draft, in which the Doctor took the dead Ashildr to the world of the witch-like coven, the Sisterhood of Karn, to see if they could resurrect her[259]. Again, the emphasis is on a 'narrative of difference', a curiosity of a character who scarcely fits into rigid gender roles. Rather than perpetuating the stereotype that queer or magical Trickster women are villainous witches, however (see, e.g., the sorceress Skade in **The Last Kingdom**, feared by almost every male character; or **Doctor Who**'s own Carrionite Mothers, 'man-eating lesbians who use magic against men'[260]), she is a considerably more complex figure, coloured in shades of light and dark.

---

[257] *Vǫluspá*, stanza 23 (Larrington, *The Poetic Edda*, p6).

[258] See also Willa and Old Ma Twiston from *The Witchfinders*, who are similarly viewed with suspicion because of their skill with herbal remedies, traditional medicine, and folkloric or pagan incantations.

[259] TCH #81, p96.

[260] Burke, Jessica, '**Doctor Who** and the Valkyrie Tradition, Part 2: Goddesses, Battle-Demons, Witches, & Wives', in Burdge et al, *The Mythological Dimensions of Doctor Who*, p146.

Ultimately, there is an identifiable subtext of queering or feminising otherwise masculine spaces at the heart of *The Girl Who Died*. This manifests in various forms: most obviously in devoting a story about Vikings – those most notoriously 'manly' warriors of the public imagination – not to valorising a form of toxic masculine behaviour but instead to a young girl with a head full of stories. Furthermore, Ashildr can plausibly be read as having a genderqueer identity, one echoing such identities in the corpus of Old Norse-Icelandic literature. Other small moments could be mentioned – a Viking man is dubbed 'Heidi' in jest because of his double-plaited beard, although he is also depicted as a cowardly shrinking violet who cannot cope with the sight of blood, which adds a problematic undertone. The key remaining example, however, is that of Clara.

The extent to which Clara constitutes meaningful representation of bisexuality (and correspondingly of queerness) across her two-and-a-half seasons in the programme is outside of the scope of this book, although most such evidence prior to *The Girl Who Died* is rooted in brief asides[261]. That continues here somewhat with the following exchange, beginning after Ashildr bids both characters good night:

CLARA

You've made an impact there.

[261] E.g., her comments about Jane Austen in *The Magician's Apprentice* and *Face the Raven*, or her echo-self Oswin mentioning her first crush, Nina, in *Asylum of the Daleks*.

DOCTOR

Stop it.

CLARA

She's nice. Fight you for her.

DOCTOR

The human race, you're obsessed. You all need to get a hobby.

CLARA

I've got a hobby, thanks. It's you, by the way.

This exchange, added shortly before the episode readthrough by Moffat[262], echoes a similar conversation in *Under the Lake* which also compared relationships to 'hobbies' and referred to them as a prevailing human obsession. This strengthens the sense that Clara's comment '[I'll] fight you for her' indicates a romantic or flirtatious interest in Ashildr on her part. By *Hell Bent*, the pair are setting sail together in a stolen TARDIS to see the universe, in an ending Moffat has at least once referred to as having a fairly clear lesbian reading[263].

There is another possible reading, however, and it is one rooted in Clara's wider arc of ascension to Doctorhood. The Doctor's female companion getting to take on something equivalent to the lead

---

[262] TCH #81, p99.

[263] Moffat, Steven, Instagram comment, '...ran off with a space lesbian. Twice,' referring to both Clara and Bill's endings during his time on **Doctor Who**.

male role in the series prefigures and paves the way for the programme's ultimate 'feminising of a masculine space', the casting of Jodie Whittaker as the first female Doctor. This was a prominent aspect of Mathieson's previous script *Flatline* (2014), in which Clara took on the Doctor mantle in various ways, and to a lesser extent it recurs here in the scene in which Clara confronts the Mire on board their spaceship. One critic has called her behaviour here a 'note-perfect'[264] impersonation of the Doctor; and indeed, she is at her most Doctor-like, exuding confidence, making whip-smart deductions, and using words as weapons like every good mercurial Trickster should. Notably, in this scene, Ashildr is cast in the role of **Clara's** companion, at first hiding behind her and then stepping forward to make a bold and arguably foolhardy gesture like many a companion before her. She is more Clara's companion than the Doctor's, which naturally foreshadows the two stealing a TARDIS and flying off to see the stars at the conclusion of *Hell Bent*.

In this light, Clara's offer to 'fight' the Doctor 'for' Ashildr is perhaps less explicitly romantic so much as it showcases Clara making a claim to the Doctor's usual territory by competing with him for the right to a new companion. This still contributes to the story's undertone of queerness, however: Clara and the Doctor's exchange echoes something Elizabeth Sandifer identifies as 'a staple scene of the new series – the seduction of the new companion (and both [Russell T] Davies and Moffat always write it as a seduction)'[265].

---

[264] Smith?, *Who Is the Doctor 2*, p182.

[265] Sandifer, Elizabeth, 'Time Can Be Rewritten: "Night of the Doctor"'. For a classic series example, see also the same author's *TARDIS Eruditorum: An Unofficial Critical History of Doctor Who*

This is not to say that every such scene of the Doctor inviting a companion on board the TARDIS is explicitly romantic; but the possibility of romantic undertones (an older male figure inviting a younger woman to travel with him) is invariably present in the tension of such scenes. Clara never really actively 'seduces' (in as family-friendly a manner as that word can be used) Ashildr into joining her on board the TARDIS. But raising the possibility of her having the power to do so implicitly positions Clara as a Doctor-analogue and amounts to a symbolic queering of this already quasi-romantic set-up. *The Girl Who Died* is only one data point along the way of Clara's queer identity and ascension to Doctorhood, but nonetheless a significant one.

4.3: 'The Universe is Full of Testosterone. Trust Me, it's Unbearable.'

For all the above symbolism and clear focus on the title character, that *The Girl Who Died* is still such a male-dominated story whilst striving to reject toxic masculinity is arguably its biggest flaw, even if it does help create the atmosphere of overwhelming testosterone about which Clara complains. Earlier drafts featured many more women, some as Valkyries and others as kidnap victims at the behest of 'Odin' who wanted to keep them for 'artificial insemination' (yet another trace, albeit unsurprisingly removed, of the story's focus on disturbing male behaviour)[266]. Also included was explicit discourse about feminism, with Ashildr originally 'a female armourer in a village where the women were slowly

---

Volume 3: Jon Pertwee, p316.
[266] TCH #81, p86.

becoming aware of gender equality' who, at Clara's encouragement, gained the strength to stand up to her abusive husband and become 'the first feminist Viking'[267]. One draft even referred to political activist Emmeline Pankhurst in dialogue, presumably to assure the Vikings that women could fight for a cause they believed in[268].

None of this made the final cut: in the story as broadcast, female villagers are rarely seen, heard, or even mentioned, feminism is not explicitly discussed, and no women are credited as cast members aside from Coleman and Williams[269]. This is a pity; to some extent it works against the agenda of replacing toxic masculinity with a different, healthier, and more admirable mode of being. One could imagine a scenario of the women of the village being the hapless fighters the Doctor must train up, although such women needing the patriarchal figure of the Doctor to teach them how to defend themselves might itself have had awkwardly patronising implications.

There **is** one other girl in this story, however: the unnamed baby who plays a surprisingly crucial role[270]. Let's call her 'the Girl Who Cried'. The idea that the Doctor is capable of understanding the precise meanings behind babies' wails ('he speaks Baby') started off as a gag in stories such as *A Good Man Goes to War* and *Closing*

---

[267] TCH #81, pp88-89.

[268] TCH #81, pp91, 94.

[269] TCH #81 lists nine uncredited female performers playing villagers, a musician, and the wife of 'Lofty' (p127), but they are only fleetingly glimpsed in the final product.

[270] 'What's **it** saying?' Clara asks of the baby, to which the Doctor responds, '**She**. She's afraid' (emphasis mine).

Time (both 2011) but is here played relatively straight and with no small amount of pathos. In purely mechanical plotting terms, the Girl Who Cried has an outsized impact far beyond her brief appearance – first, her cries convince the Doctor to stay and save the villagers, and secondly, her cryptic reference to 'fire in the water' (a reasonable approximation of an infant's understanding of electric eels) provides a key piece of the jigsaw in terms of defeating the Mire.

However, the Girl Who Cried does not **just** possess a plot function. As provider of an enigmatic riddle that needs solving, her counterpart in Norse mythology terms would be a 'vǫlva': a wise woman, or seeress, and usually an old woman at that[271]. That in this case the riddle comes from an infant who cannot yet speak is a clever and characteristically comical inversion of the sort of figure, defined by the power of their words, who would normally dispense such advice: yet another iteration of the story's insistence on interrogating what one sees, looking beyond the obvious. Secondly, her cries prompt the Doctor's poignant musing 'do babies die with honour?', constituting an effective challenge to Einarr's idealised dream of dying in battle and by extension the Viking warrior ethos.

The Doctor's translations of this baby's frightened cries (printed in full in the Appendix) add a rich vein of lyricism to a story that otherwise features no direct instances of oral poetry or recitation. As counterpoint to the Viking rapacity of the popular cultural imagination, the Norse talent for 'verbal skills' points to a society

[271] The term is interchangeable with 'spákerling', 'old prophecy woman'.

that was often 'civilised and intelligent'[272]. This contrast between brutality and profound emotional expression is one the programme has itself highlighted in characterising the Ice Warriors as being 'like the Vikings', on the basis that they could 'slaughter whole civilisations, yet weep at the crushing of a flower'[273]. Again, it is typically, iconoclastically **Doctor Who**ish that the closest the episode gets to Norse poetry comes not from a 'skáld' or poet, but a baby girl[274]. The vast majority of such skalds were male, and at least one of the four or so named women skalds known to us was 'a favourite hate-figure of the Icelandic saga-writers'[275], damningly depicted elsewhere in the literature – so Norse society's lyrical side manifesting in the Girl Who Cried is yet another inversion of conventional Viking Age gender roles.

Curiously, the mother whom the baby addresses in her speech (as translated by the Doctor) is both absent and silent; presumably she is still around, if the baby girl is speaking directly to her. Her absence is thus a bit of an oddity that gets no satisfactory explanation; could she not have been the parent swaddling the infant rather than her father? It would entail sacrificing the gag about Brot/'Lofty' having 'been at it hammer and tongs' because he is a father as well as a blacksmith, but this seems a fairly small loss. That said, the fact that the village blacksmith – one of the

---

[272] Faulkes, Anthony, *Poetical Inspiration in Old Norse and Old English Poetry*, p31.
[273] *Empress of Mars*.
[274] See the Appendix for further discussion of the baby's 'speech' in relation to Norse poetry.
[275] Jesch, *Women in the Viking Age*, p161.

professions most associated with masculinity in Norse society[276] – is also portrayed as a loving and attentive father clearly contributes to the story's overall agenda of highlighting positive alternatives to a certain brand of stereotypical male behaviour[277]. It is therefore something of a shame that the Doctor refers to Brot/'Lofty' as the baby's 'junior parent': no doubt intended as little more than a characteristically Moffat joke about how men are rubbish, but with the awkward connotation that fatherhood involves less responsibility or commitment than motherhood.

Instead of devoting the runtime to exploring the experiences of various women in the village, the focus is instead on a recurring Moffat-era theme: with the right blend of silliness and queerness as political action in the face of toxicity, as well as actually listening to women and ceding ground in conventionally masculine spheres, men can become good people and such toxicity can be defeated. This is an extremely worthy aim and valuable message. But the story is still in large part about these men – or really about one man in particular: the Doctor. Ashildr may be the title character of this particular episode, but there is an inexorable gravity exerted by the title character of the entire show, and even here she is only granted 32 lines of dialogue. It is clear that more remains to be said about her life and her experiences, with the story's final minutes

---

[276] Jesch goes as far as to say 'about the only implements found exclusively in the graves of one sex are blacksmith's tools in male graves' (*Women in the Viking Age*, p21).

[277] For another touching example of male sensitivity and vulnerability presented in a positive fashion, see the moment in which Einarr admits tearily that he lacks the strength to keep his daughter safe.

setting up just such an opportunity. Thankfully, scriptwriters Catherine Tregenna and Sarah Dollard – the first women to write for televised **Doctor Who** since 2008 – go on to do exactly that in the next two episodes in which Ashildr appears.

CHAPTER 5: TELLING A BETTER STORY

Throughout this book a number of elements have been running alongside each other in parallel: toxic masculinity, overt farce, Óðinn's mythological role as trickster-healer, and transgressive femininity. This concluding chapter illustrates how these seemingly disparate threads all align perfectly in the conclusion to *The Girl Who Died* in a manner very specific to it being a **Doctor Who** story, arguing for the fundamental nature of such stories as being better than other kinds on offer. Lastly, the second half of this chapter will deal with the more disquieting coda that follows this triumphant resolution, and the pleasing note of ambiguity it adds to the story while teasing what is to come the following week.

5.1: 'You've Just Seen the World Through the Eyes of a Storyteller'

The two key terms first mentioned in the Introduction – apotropaic laughter and soteriological trickery – are on display in full force in the denouement of *The Girl Who Died*. In short, evil is dispatched by both the power of humour and the power of illusions, acting in tandem. Without the illusory monster generated by Ashildr's imagination, there would be no chance of publicly mocking the Mire. Without weaponising their blatant ridiculousness against them, the deception would only hold them off for a few minutes before they would presumably return, confident of not actually having to face a gigantic serpent.

One of the cleverest aspects of this conclusion is that the Mire are both intimidated and made to look ridiculous by something intrinsically connected to **Doctor Who** in public discourse: a very fake-looking special effect[278]. The audience is shown something that is intended to be scary, but which fails to successfully sell the illusion and ends up being laughable instead – a common criticism of the programme in its 20th-century run and even occasionally in its 21st-century iteration[279]. In this instance, the questionable special effect is a carved wooden representation of a beast described variously as a 'giant serpent-like creature', a 'sea-serpent', and (most commonly) a 'dragon'[280].

This moment echoes one of the series' most infamously poor bits of FX. Seasoned fans will immediately think of *Kinda* (1982), in which the ending's giant snake looked so rubbery that it was re-rendered using CGI for the DVD release. As with the way humour often works, there is a huge gulf between the way things seem to – or are supposed to – be (the fearsome Mara, demonic inhabitants of the Places of the Inside) and the way they are actually realised (a big rubber snake). This should not be taken as a criticism of 20th-century **Doctor Who** as such: these sorts of effects were done on the cheap, but they served their purpose at the time, frightening or thrilling children and indeed inspiring many of them to grow up to

---

[278] This is not the first time a Mathieson script has included an in-joke about classic **Who**'s low budget: in *Mummy on the Orient Express*, Clara is relieved to find that an ominous sarcophagus is, in fact, 'full of bubble wrap', in a nod to the memorable means by which the effects department conveyed Wirrn metamorphosis in *The Ark in Space* (1975).

[279] E.g., Warner, Terry, 'Doctor Who: 10 Special Effects That Totally Sucked' (the snake in *Kinda* ranks at #5).

[280] TCH #81, pp83, 112, 94-5, Cooper, *Steven Moffat's Doctor Who*, p157; Rollason, *The Girl Who Died*, pp33-34, and Mathieson in Arnopp, 'Immortal Words', DWM #493.

work in television.

Crucially, though, the very shoddiness of the wooden serpent effect is key to why this soteriological trickery works. If it were more convincing, the situation (and the footage) would not be nearly as humorous, and so the Mire would not flee in disgrace. In other words, the story is not merely making a joke at the expense of classic **Doctor Who**'s low budget. It is **actively celebrating** the power of the poor special effect within a good story, which acts as metonym for the programme as a whole – as something fundamentally silly and charming, but which nonetheless captures the imagination and can make a material difference in the real world. In short, it is delighting in getting to be a story that can only be a **Doctor Who** story and nothing else – and, explicitly given the discourse of the poor special effect, one that is told through the medium of television. A better Way of Viewing, as it were.

The whole episode takes a kind of giddy delight in the sheer fact of its being a **Doctor Who** story, doing the sort of bizarre and incongruous juxtapositions only this programme can really do in its Pythonesque state of postmodern melange. Various critics' positive feedback took much the same line: one reviewer wrote, 'this is doughty, bassline [sic] […] **Doctor Who** 101'[281], while another called it 'the quintessential **Doctor Who** story' –for the first 35 minutes at least[282]. They're not wrong. Throughout the sequence of the Doctor and company formulating their plan and defeating the Mire, a combination of explicit silliness, illusions with moral force

---

[281] Kibble-White, Graham, 'The DWM Review: *The Girl Who Died*', DWM #493.
[282] Smith?, *Who Is the Doctor 2,* p181.

behind them, and the rich imaginative potential of a young, genderqueer woman repels the excesses of toxic masculinity increasingly associated with the far right. It is a perfect summary of the sort of thing this programme stands for.

That the episode's resolution acts as so decisive a championing of the ethos of **Doctor Who** is fitting, given that throughout its runtime it flirts with entertaining a very different ethos. From its title onward, *The Girl Who Died* defines itself by, is almost haunted by, the prospect of a very grim ending in which a promising guest character is killed off. That it is set in the medieval world – which decades of popular culture have taught audiences to associate with grimness, gritty realism, and violence – makes this seem yet more plausible. It sets out its stall early on as dealing with warfare and conflict, as well as the futility of going up against a much more powerful enemy one cannot hope to defeat by force alone. This is a classic 'valiant last stand' situation – indicating the likelihood of noble sacrifices, desperate choices, and subsequent lamentations for the dead. Mathieson has indicated that earlier versions of the episode leaned into this ethos more whole-heartedly, calling them 'dark and quite tortured, like a nihilistic meditation on death', and describing the Doctor's training up of the Viking warriors as 'almost assisted suicide'[283].

As if that were not enough, *The Girl Who Died* boasts Maisie Williams in its guest cast, one of the most recognisable stars from what was, at the time, almost certainly the biggest medievalist show in the world. Even if Williams was not cast due to her performance on **Game of Thrones**, it was a terrific stroke of

---

[283] Mathieson in Arnopp, 'Immortal Words', DWM #493.

serendipity that she was offered and accepted this particular guest role. Ashildr and Arya are not especially similar as characters, outside of both being plucky young adventurer-heroines in a medieval setting and both being played by Maisie Williams[284]. Ashildr is considerably more untested, more tentative, less hardened; although she is 'strange', she is still a key part of her community, as opposed to Arya who is often defined by her outsider-hood. But the fact remains that, in 2015, at the peak of **Game of Thrones**' cultural footprint, Arya was enormously prominent in audiences' minds when Williams appeared on **Doctor Who** as another medieval heroine.

Thus, the episode is at the paratextual level inviting comparisons with **Game of Thrones**.

Among other things, the HBO behemoth is particularly renowned for its capacity for bloodthirstiness. In contemporary cultural perception at least, no character was safe, no matter how beloved: any could be killed off at a moment's notice[285]. Indeed, when *The Girl Who Died* aired, Jon Snow, one of **Thrones**' most significant characters, had just been stabbed to death in the shocking Season 5 finale. His resurrection (which did rather permanent damage to the show's reputation for grimdark bloodthirstiness[286]) came about at the start of the following season. By flirting with the paratextual

---

[284] There is, though, a cheeky nod to **Thrones**' oft-repeated phrase 'winter is coming' in *Hell Bent*, in which Williams delivers the line 'summer can't last forever'.

[285] Jeffery, Morgan, '**Game of Thrones** Exec: "No One is Safe"'.

[286] Alston, Trey, 'On **Game of Thrones**, No One was Safe – Now Everyone Is'.

paraphernalia of **Game of Thrones** (swords and sorcery, medieval villages, plucky adventurer-heroines, Maisie Williams) in a story specifically signposting that a girl will die, **Doctor Who** is openly teasing that it might go down the HBO route of hard-hitting brutality.

This is common to how the programme works under Steven Moffat's tenure as showrunner; Sandifer has identified his penchant for what she calls 'narrative substitution'[287]. In brief, this involves dramatic tension over what kind of story is being told: teetering on the edge of committing to a certain set of principles or tropes, and then firmly committing to swapping those principles or tropes out for a different set[288]. The general idea is that the substitution is in aid of telling a better story – rejecting certain familiar items in the storyteller's arsenal and going beyond them to do something a little more surprising and unexpected, something which has a solid claim to being morally or ideologically superior. Naturally, this runs the risk of alienating certain sections of the audience who have a strong preference for the rejected kind of story, but that is the inherently prickly and risky – and therefore fascinating – game that narrative substitution is playing. It could also be argued that it is excessively didactic or sermonising, in teaching viewers that story template A is better than B; even that it is hypocritical, in using B to lure people in only to tell them off for wanting to see B in the first place. These are fair complaints, and it is certainly understandable why this approach does not work for

[287] Sandifer, 'Make Me a Warrior Now (*A Good Man Goes to War*)'.
[288] Arguably its most explicit manifestation is the Doctor's declaration in *Hide* (2013) that 'This isn't a ghost story, it's a love story!'

everyone. But for those who appreciate these sorts of metatextual games Moffat is playing with his genre-savvy audience, it can make for dizzyingly thrilling television.

Narrative substitution is exactly what is going on in *The Girl Who Died*, itself a story that is particularly conscious of and interested in storytelling. The signs are there that this will be a story about the clash of Viking and Mire masculinities, involving lots of violence and bloodshed, and that Ashildr will die tragically at the end. That her death will ultimately achieve little more than to spark the self-obsessed misery of the male lead, placing it firmly in the 'fridging' trope whereby women are props to be killed off primarily to initiate the development of self-serious 'manpain'[289]. That our brooding, dark antihero will offer a trite platitude posing as a grim truth, like 'there should've been another way' or 'the monsters and I are not so different', and the credits will roll. That, finally, think-pieces will pop up rapidly online about how the show 'failed Maisie Williams', echoing the sorts of criticism that became increasingly common with regard to misogynist writing choices in **Game of Thrones**, to the point that Williams herself voiced surprise and frustration with regard to her character[290].

Instead, this ethos is wholly rejected by embracing a sillier and

---

[289] See, e.g., Simone, Gail, 'Women in Refrigerators'; Eva Dagbjört Óladóttir, 'The Privilege of Pain: "Manpain" and the Suffering Hero in the **Supernatural** Series'.

[290] Smith, SE, '**Game of Thrones**' Fantasy Misogyny'; Bruney, Gabrielle, '**Game of Thrones**'s Treatment of Women Will Tarnish Its Legacy'; Carr, Mary Kate, 'Maisie Williams Was "Surprised" by That **Game of Thrones** Sex Scene – Because She Thought Arya Was Queer'.

queerer story. A story about translating the babble of babies; a story about electric eels, puppets, and laughter. A symbolic stand is taken against the sort of stories associated with **Game of Thrones**, by hijacking its broadly familiar template (and even one of its cast members) and asserting that, no, the ethos of **Doctor Who** makes this fundamentally **better**. It was something Mathieson himself had to learn: 'I was trying to avoid a rompy episode,' he said of the writing process, 'but my instinct there was wrong'[291]. As Darren Mooney puts it, the episode 'rejects the brutality and violence associated with the world of **Game of Thrones**' and 'suggests that the best way to escape a grim story is to simply construct a new one'[292].

This narrative substitution is not merely a switch or a fake-out, but part of an active discourse around storytelling. Ashildr is labelled 'a storyteller' who is in the habit of making up stories about the men of her village coming home safely, with the goal that this will affect the real outcome. In other words, she dreams a better reality and hopes to make it manifest, which is how all radical change starts. The climax of this plot thread is filtered through the imagination of a young person, in tune with the recurring motif – especially common in Moffat's **Who** – of idealising the wonder with which children view the world[293]. It is her imagination that provides 'a

---

[291] Mathieson in Arnopp, 'Immortal Words', DWM #493.

[292] Mooney, '**Doctor Who**: *The Girl Who Died* (Review)'.

[293] E.g., the idea that growing up (and losing one's childlike sense of wonder) is something the Doctor can 'fix' (*The Eleventh Hour*); seven-year-old Amelia Pond's persevering belief in stars even in a universe that has gone dark without them (*The Big Bang*); and the sentimental idea that children can hear the Doctor's real name 'if

story [the Mire will] never forget': the ethos of **Doctor Who**.

That ethos? A genderqueer girl, who does not fit in but loves storytelling, possesses the ability to win out over the stories of a hyper-masculine hegemony by coming up with her own. She shatters the narrative tyranny of tropes and familiar structures bound by rigid, inflexible parameters, and dares to imagine something bold and emancipatory.

5.2: 'The Story's Not Over Yet'

...and then Ashildr dies.

It is impressive that this fact feels surprising and wrong, somehow, given that it comes at the climax of a story called *The Girl Who Died*; the audience has hardly been cheated. Yet something about the anarchic, gleeful romp that the story has been for 35 minutes – a story that deliberately feels low-stakes and disposable in many ways – allows viewers to momentarily forget that the story must end this way. That the girl must die, to paraphrase **Game of Thrones**. As a result, when Ashildr is found to be dead, there is a sense both of surprise at the sudden tonal shift from merriment and silliness towards doom and gloom, but also of inevitability, as the story fulfils its well-signposted brief. The Doctor has saved the day but, as Mathieson put it, 'there's always a cost'[294].

The previous chapter compared Ashildr to the maiden-kings of Old Norse-Icelandic literature. In the rímur poems, these figures are allowed to transgress conventional gender roles and break out of

---

their hearts are in the right place' (*Twice Upon a Time*).

[294] Mathieson in Arnopp, 'Episode Preview'.

their social and narrative constraints for a brief period. But 'normal service' is invariably resumed at the end, returning such characters to the meek demureness of womanhood after they have been conquered or humiliated by a male suitor. Ashildr's situation does not completely map onto this, but there is an echo of it in the fact that she dies while wearing a bulky, metallic, masculine-coded object: a Mire helmet. The narrative teeters on the edge of punishing her for her transgression and her hubris, much as the programme will feign at doing with Clara, later in the season.

As with Clara, a narrative substitution takes place. The tired trope of the 'fridged' woman that the episode comes perilously close to indulging in is ultimately rejected when the Doctor resurrects Ashildr. The price to pay is seemingly averted. Self-introspection and a moment of anagnorisis lead the Doctor to discover something within himself, something fundamental about who he is, and he embraces the role of Odinic healer that means he can bring Ashildr back from death. Again, the kind of story *The Girl Who Died* has briefly threatened to be is abandoned in favour of one regarded as morally or ideologically better – full of greater optimism, compassion, and less of a frustrating dead-end masquerading as profundity.

The gears change once again, however, and the episode closes in a sombre, disquieting fashion. Yes, the day has been saved. And yes, the Doctor has successfully revived Ashildr, archetypal trickster-healer that he is. But in the final scenes the tone is one of foreboding rather than triumph; for the last time, the story shifts between its two predominant registers, ending on something more ambiguous and sophisticated than might be expected given its earlier, romp-like nature.

Almost immediately, the Doctor seems to experience regret over what he has done. He predicts Ashildr will see him again in the future 'once she understands' exactly what his actions have meant for her. He is already thinking ahead to how she will feel the unbearable pain and loss that come with being immortal, and the fact that rather than living forever it merely feels like 'everybody else dying'; he tries to plan for this by giving her a second Mire medical kit which she can give to 'someone she can't bear to lose'. Clara, noticing his brooding, says that 'silence is even worse in a Scottish accent', a direct echo of a comment made at a particularly spooky and foreboding moment the previous season: 'Do you have your own mood lighting now? Because, frankly, the accent is enough'[295]. Now he can think more clearly, the Doctor recognises that he was 'emotional' and 'angry', and that he might have made a 'terrible mistake... maybe even a tidal wave'. Lastly, the final sequence, representing how years, decades, and centuries will pass for Ashildr, sees the expression on her face shifting from one of serenity and joy at being alive to increasing distress, grief, and eventually quiet rage – the closing shot of the episode.

Resurrecting Ashildr will indeed have huge ramifications for the rest of the season. In some ways it is a classical arc of hubris: the Doctor taking it upon himself to confer immortality on another ends up directly leading to the death of his best friend and his loss of all memory of her[296]. If he had not resurrected Ashildr, she would clearly never have been in a position to make a deal with the Time Lords or use a quantum shade – and Clara would not have

---

[295] *Listen*.
[296] Until those memories are regained in *Twice Upon a Time*.

died, at least not there and then. The words 'emotional' and 'angry' to describe his mental state here perfectly describe his reaction to Clara's death and foreshadow how far he will go to save her in *Hell Bent*; the lengths to which he goes there are also clearly a source of unease within the narrative.

Additionally, later episodes make it clear that Ashildr feels conflicted at best and negative at worst about her newfound immortality. The curse of living a long life and losing those you care about is a key theme of the 2015 season, with various episodes dwelling on the Doctor's feelings about the prospect of losing Clara. Accordingly, *The Woman Who Lived* delivers a stinging rebuttal to the Doctor's actions, as Ashildr (now calling herself 'Me') tells him that rather than saving her life, he 'trapped [her] inside it'; we get glimpses of the terrible losses she has sustained in the 800 years since her resurrection. In keeping with the wider season's interest in complex, hybridic figures who are simultaneously friend and enemy, both good and bad for you, she becomes half-antagonist, half-ally.

The question, then, is whether ending on this sombre note undoes the previous triumphs. Surely the argument in favour of soteriological trickery and Odinic healing no longer stands, if there is clearly such ambiguity about it in the text itself? The Doctor may proclaim that 'I'm the Doctor, and I save people!' but does this episode not challenge his modus operandi?

This ending does not so much undo as complicate the overall message. After all, Clara proclaims – and we are well-accustomed to regarding the Doctor's companions as moral centres of the narrative, even if they are not infallible – that 'Whatever [the

Doctor] did for Ashildr, she deserved it'. She deserved life, the episode decides, and the right to continue her story, even if that story will definitely include both pain and loss. Ashildr clearly resents the Doctor for a time because of what he did to her, but after a phase as an enemy she goes on to become a friend. She weaves herself into the fabric of history; she saves lives, curing an entire village of scarlet fever; and she goes on to run a refugee camp for aliens stuck on Earth, a sanctuary 'with strict laws against violence'[297]. In the end, she becomes Clara's companion, travelling the stars with her in a stolen TARDIS, in an ending that clearly takes joy in Clara's ascension to the Doctor role and Ashildr's presence at her side. It is ultimately hard to read Series 9 as arguing that Ashildr living a long, immortal life is unambiguously bad.

Come the finale to the season, Clara is effectively placed in the same newly-resurrected, newly-immortal position. In both cases, the moral conclusion seems to be that these resurrections are not morally wrong things to have happened in and of themselves, **but also** that the Doctor goes too far in setting himself up in the position of implementing them. As such, there is a pleasingly nuanced ambivalence towards the idea of Doctor-as-Óðinn. On a good day, the character might save your town with the goofiest of schemes; on a bad one, they'll trap you inside your prolonged life until the end of time; some days they might even do both. This perfectly reflects not only the series' willingness to explore its hero from all angles, but also Norse mythology's own understanding of Óðinn as a richly flawed character.

In the end, *The Girl Who Died* reaches a kind of synthesis between

---

[297] *Face the Raven.*

its diametrically opposed modes of narrative that have formed the backbone of this book. Throughout its runtime, it has entertained the possibility of being a gritty and bloodthirsty medievalist story, whilst reliably coming down on the side of something much sillier and queerer, using apotropaic laughter, soteriological trickery, and a profound and unembarrassed love of being **Doctor Who** to banish toxic masculinity. To kill off Ashildr is the natural conclusion to the former, which is toyed with but wholeheartedly rejected. To resurrect her in the neatest and tidiest of happy endings and waltz off to the TARDIS like nothing has happened, never to see her again, is arguably the natural conclusion to the latter[298].

Sometimes you do not have to choose between two bad choices. *The Girl Who Died* threads the needle between both of these, setting up a four-episode arc that sees this immortal young woman grow and change over the span of millennia. She is neither a promising guest star cut down in service of a cheap shock, nor a character given a trite and pat happy-ever-after that feels emotionally insincere. Instead, the series will go on to examine what it means for her to continue living, what it means for her to suffer the burden of an immeasurably long life. As she might put it, that life will be sad, and it will be beautiful. Perhaps the best place to end her story is after the end itself.

---

[298] For an existing **Doctor Who** example that somewhat follows this pattern, see the treatment of Jenny in *The Doctor's Daughter* (2008).

APPENDIX: BABY TALK

To what extent does the 'speech' of the baby, as translated by the Doctor, really echo the cadence and metre of Old Norse poetry, as has been claimed[299]? The full speech as it is spoken in the programme is reproduced below. Regular prose which does not resemble any known meter from Old Norse poetry is presented in plain text; alliteration and consonance (repetition of consonant sounds) are marked in bold. It should be noted that in early Germanic languages such as Old Norse all vowels could alliterate with each other. Each line is followed by a note about its number of syllables, and then its number of stressed or emphasised syllables (also known as 'lifts').

There is one kenning present, in the two identical lines of Stanza Five: a kenning is a cryptic, riddling compound metaphor common in Norse skaldic poetry in particular, and often difficult to grasp without prior familiarity with the set phrases and networks of meaning. Half-lines are demarcated by the indented gap indicating a caesura or break in the flow of the poetry. The sections of the speech which most closely correspond to the Old Norse poetic meter of ljóðaháttr are underlined.

Stanza One

1. **I** am afr**ai**d, Mother. (six syllables, with three lifts)

2. **Ho**ld **me, Mo**ther. (four syllables, with two lifts)

3. **I** am afr**ai**d. (four syllables, with two lifts)

---

[299] By Burk and Smith? in *Who Is The Doctor 2*, p179.

Stanza Two

1. **Tu**rn your face **to**wards **me**, **M**other, (eight syllables, with four lifts)

2. For **you're**, **you're** beautiful. (six syllables, with three lifts)

3. And I w**i**ll s**i**ng for you. (six syllables, with three lifts)

4. **I** am afr**ai**d, but **I** will sing. (eight syllables, with four lifts)

Stanza Three

1. Mo**th**er, I hear **th**under. (six syllables, with three lifts)

2. Mother, I hear shouting. (six syllables, with three lifts)

3. You **are** my w**or**ld, (four syllables, with two lifts)

4. But I hear other worlds now. (seven syllables, with four lifts)

Stanza Four

1. Be**yo**nd th'unf**o**l- ding **of** **yo**ur smile, (eight syllables, with four lifts)

2. Is **th**ere o**th**er kindness? (six syllables, with three lifts)

3. **I** am afr**ai**d. Will th**ey** be **kind**? (eight syllables, with four lifts)

4. The sk**y** is cr**y**ing now. (six syllables, with three lifts)

Stanza Five

1. Fire in the water. (six syllables, with three lifts)

2. Fire in the water. (six syllables, with three lifts)

Broadly speaking, ljóðaháttr involves four-line stanzas containing long, odd-numbered lines that each comprise two half-lines (such as lines 1 and 2 in Stanza One and lines 1 and 3 in Stanza Four), alternating with shorter, even-numbered lines (line 2 in Stanzas Two and Four; line 4 in Stanza Two comes close but contains too many syllables). Long, odd-numbered lines should contain four lifts while the shorter, even-numbered ones contain only three (as in all underlined lines bar Stanza Two line 4). The third full line in a ljóðaháttr stanza should end in a stressed, monosyllabic word (as line 3 in Stanza Four indeed does – 'kind'). Lastly, odd lines can contain either two or three lifts which alliterate with each other, while even ones should contain only two; the first syllable in an odd line's first half-line should alliterate with the first syllable in the second half-line (as in line 1 of Stanza Two; the first line of Stanza Four cheats at this slightly).

My own analysis of the metrical rhythms behind the baby's words suggests that a reasonable proportion of it, if not quite all, bears some hallmarks of the ljóðaháttr verse form. Some of it is irregular or does not quite fit the rhythmic 'rules' – but that even such a proportion comes close to imitating a (to lay viewers) fairly obscure form of poetry is in itself quite impressive. The kenning used to refer to the electric eels, 'fire in the water', is a particularly deft choice, since it works plausibly both as a childlike way of referring to these creatures and the sort of construction used in kennings (even if 'fire of the water' would be slightly more accurate).

BIBLIOGRAPHY

Books

Andersson, Theodore M, and Kari Ellen Gade, trans, *Morkinskinna: The Earliest Icelandic Chronicle of the Norwegian Kings (1030-1157)*. Ithaca, Cornell University Press, 2000. ISBN 9780801436949.

Aristotle, *Poetics*. Fourth century BCE. SH Butcher, trans, *The Poetics of Aristotle*. London/NY, Macmillan, 1902.

Árni Björnsson, *Wagner and the Volsungs: Icelandic Sources of Der Ring des Nibelungen*. London, Viking Society for Northern Research, 2003. ISBN 9780903521555.

Arvidsson, Stefan, *Draksjukan: Mytiska Fantasier hos Tolkien, Wagner, och de Vries*. Lund, Nordic Academic Press, 2007. ISBN 9789189116931.

Bakhtin, Mikhail, *Problems of Dostoevsky's Poetics*. 1963. Caryl Emerson, trans, Minneapolis, University of Minnesota Press, 1984. **Theory and History of Literature Volume 8.** ISBN 9780816612284.

Bakhtin, Mikhail, *Rabelais and His World*. 1965. Hélène Iswolsky, trans, Bloomington, Indiana University Press, 1984. ISBN 9780253203410.

Berger, John, *Ways of Seeing*. London, Penguin Classics, 2008. ISBN 9780141035796.

Burdge, Anthony, Jessica Burke, and Kristine Larsen, eds, *The Mythological Dimensions of Doctor Who*. Crawfordville, Kitsune Books, 2010. ISBN 9780981949581.

Burke, Jessica, '**Doctor Who** and the Valkyrie Tradition, Part

2: Goddesses, Battle Demons, Wives and Daughters', pp140-83.

Hills, Matthew, '"Mythology Makes You Feel Something": The Russell T Davies Era as Sentimental Journey', pp198-215.

Burk, Graeme and Robert Smith?, *Who is the Doctor 2: The Unofficial Guide to Doctor Who – the Modern Series*[300]. Toronto, ECW Press, 2020. ISBN 9781770414150.

Butler, David, ed, *Time and Relative Dissertations in Space: Critical Perspectives on Doctor Who*. Manchester, Manchester University Press, 2007. ISBN 9780719076824.

Charles, Alec, 'The Ideology of Anachronism: Television, History and the Nature of Time', pp108-22.

O'Mahony, Daniel, '"Now How is That Wolf Able to Impersonate a Grandmother?" History, Pseudo-History and Genre in *Doctor Who*', pp56-67.

Rafer, David, 'Mythic Identity in *Doctor Who*', pp123-37.

Wood, Tat, 'The Empire of the Senses: Narrative Form and Point-of-View in **Doctor Who**', pp89-107.

Charles, Alec, *Out of Time: The Deaths and Resurrection of Doctor Who*. Oxford, Peter Lang, 2015. ISBN 9783034319416.

Clark, David, and Carl Phelpstead, eds, *Old Norse Made New: Essays on the Post-Medieval Reception of Old Norse Literature and*

[300] Stacey Smith? has requested she be credited as 'Robert' when citing her earlier work.

Culture. London, Viking Society for Northern Research, 2007. ISBN 9780903521765.

Clark, David, 'Old Norse Made New: Past and Present in Modern Children's Literature', pp133-51.

Fimi, Dimitra, 'Tolkien and Old Norse Antiquity: Real and Romantic Links in Material Culture', pp83-99.

Connell, Raewyn, *Masculinities*. Sydney, Allen & Unwin, 1995. ISBN 9780745634272.

Cooper, Steven, *Steven Moffat's Doctor Who 2014-2015: The Critical Fan's Guide to Peter Capaldi's Doctor (Unauthorized)*. Cambridge, Punked Books, 2016. ISBN 9781908375315.

Cornell, Paul, *Timewyrm: Revelation*. **Virgin New Adventures**. London, Virgin Books, 1991. ISBN 9780426203605.

Evans, DAH, ed, *Hávamál*. London, Viking Society for Northern Research, 2017. ISBN 9780903521956.

Evans, Gareth Lloyd, and Jessica Clare Hancock, eds, *Masculinities in Old Norse Literature*. Cambridge, D. S. Brewer, 2020. ISBN 9781787448193.

Lavender, Philip, 'Vulnerable Masculinities and the Vicissitudes of Power in *Göngu-Hrólfs saga*', pp97-112.

Falk, Hjalmar, *Odensheite*. Biri, Blåkoll Forlag, 2018. ISBN 9788299988124.

Faulkes, Anthony, *Poetical Inspiration in Old Norse and Old English Poetry*. London, Viking Society for Northern Research, 1997. ISBN 9780903521321.

Finch, RG, ed and trans, *Vǫlsunga saga: The Saga of the Volsungs*. London/Edinburgh, Nelson, 1965.

Franke, Alyssa, *Hell Bent*. **The Black Archive** #22. Edinburgh, Obverse Books, 2018. ISBN 9781909031715.

Fugelso, Karl, ed, *Politics and Medievalism*. **Studies in Medievalism XXIX.** Cambridge, DS Brewer, 2020. ISBN 9781843845560.

Vishnuvajjala, Usha, 'Objectivity, Impossibility and Laughter in **Doctor Who**'s *Robot of Sherwood*', pp201-15.

Goeres, Erin Michelle, *The Poetics of Commemoration: Skaldic Verse and Social Memory, c890-1070.* Oxford, Oxford University Press, 2015. ISBN 9780198745747.

Grammaticus, Saxo, *The Nine Books of the Danish History of Saxo Grammaticus in Two Volumes* (*Gesta Danorum*). 12th century. Oliver Elton, trans, London/New York, Norrœna Society, 1905.

Groenewegen, Sarah, *Face the Raven.* **The Black Archive** #20. Edinburgh, Obverse Books, 2018. ISBN 9781909031692.

Guðbrandur Vigfússon, *Origines Islandicae: A Collection of the More Important Sagas and Other Native Writings Relating to the Settlement and Early History of Iceland*, Vol II. Oxford, Clarendon Press, 1905. Republished: London, Forgotten Books, 2015. ISBN 9781331912422.

Hansen, Christopher J, ed, *Ruminations, Peregrinations and Regenerations: A Critical Approach to Doctor Who*. Cambridge, Cambridge Scholars Publishing, 2010. ISBN 9781443820844.

O'Day, Andrew, 'Towards a Definition of Satire in *Doctor Who*', pp264-82.

Hastrup, Kirsten, ed, *Other Histories*. **European Association of Social Anthropologists**. London, Routledge, 1992. ISBN 9780415061223.

Hastrup, Kirsten, 'Uchronia and the Two Histories of Iceland, 1400-1800', pp102-20.

Hermann Pálsson and Paul Edwards, ed and trans, *Göngu-Hrolf's Saga: A Viking Romance*. Edinburgh, Canongate, 1980. ISBN 9780903937955.

Hermann Pálsson and Paul Edwards, ed and trans, *Seven Viking Romances*. London, Penguin, 1985. ISBN 9780140444742.

Hertzler, Joyce O, *Laughter: A Socio-Scientific Analysis*. New York, Exposition Press, 1970. ISBN 9780682471183.

Höckert, Robert, *Vǫluspá och vanakulten*. Uppsala, Almqvist and Wiksell, 1930.

Hollander, Lee M, *Old Norse Poems: The Most Important Non-Skaldic Verse Not Included in the Poetic Edda*. New York, Columbia University Press, 1936. ISBN 9780231921848.

Jarman, Cat, *River Kings: The Vikings from Scandinavia to the Silk Roads*. London, HarperCollins, 2021. ISBN 9780008353117.

Jesch, Judith, *Women in the Viking Age*. Woodbridge, Boydell & Brewer Ltd, 1991. ISBN 9780851153605.

Jochens, Jenny, *Women in Old Norse Society*. Ithaca/London, Cornell University Press, 1995. ISBN 9780801485207.

Kilburn, Matthew, *The Time Warrior*. **The Black Archive** #24. Edinburgh, Obverse Books, 2018. ISBN 9781909031753.

Lacan, Jacques, *Écrits*. 1966. Bruce Fink, trans, New York, WW Norton & Company, 2007. ISBN 9780393329254.

Larrington, Carolyne, ed and trans, *The Poetic Edda*. Oxford, Oxford University Press, 2014. ISBN 9780199675340.

Larrington, Carolyne, *Winter is Coming: The Medieval World of Game of Thrones*. London, I B Tauris, 2015. ISBN 9781784532567.

Lindow, John, *Norse Mythology: A Guide to Gods, Heroes, Rituals and Beliefs*. Oxford, Oxford University Press, 2002. ISBN 9780195153828.

Louis-Jensen, Jonna, Christopher Sanders, and Peter Springborg, eds, *The Sixth International Saga Conference, 28.7-28.8 1985: Workshop papers I-II*. Copenhagen, Det Arnamagnænska Institut, 1985.

Mitchell, Stephen A, '"Nú Gef ek Þik Óðni": Attitudes Toward Odin in the Mythical-Heroic Sagas', pp777-91.

Magnus Magnusson and Hermann Pálsson, *The Vinland Sagas: The Norse Discovery of America*. London, Penguin, 1965. ISBN 9780140441543.

Miles, Lawrence, and Tat Wood, *1980 to 1984: Seasons 18 to 21*. **About Time: The Unauthorized Guide to Doctor Who**. Des Moines, Mad Norwegian Press, 2010. ISBN 9780975944646.

Mooney, Darren, *Kill the Moon*. **The Black Archive** #59. Edinburgh, Obverse Books, 2022. ISBN 9781913456320.

O'Donoghue, Heather, *Old Norse-Icelandic Literature: A Short Introduction*. Oxford, Wiley/Blackwell, 2004. ISBN 9780631236269.

Örnólfur Thorsson, ed, *The Sagas of Icelanders: A Selection*.

London, Penguin, 2005. ISBN 9780141000039.

Kunz, Keneva, trans, 'The Saga of the People of Laxardal', pp270-421.

Parkin, Lance, and Lars Pearson, *AHistory: An Unauthorized History of the Doctor Who Universe*. Fourth ed, vol 1. Des Moines, Mad Norwegian Press, 2018. ISBN 9781935234227.

Poor, Sara S, and Jana K Schulman, eds, *Women in Medieval Epic: Gender, Genre and the Limits of Epic Masculinity*. London, Palgrave Macmillan, 2007. ISBN 9781349733095.

Layher, William, 'Caught Between Worlds: Gendering the Maiden Warrior in Old Norse', pp183-208.

Purser-Hallard, Philip, *Battlefield*. **The Black Archive** #34. Edinburgh, Obverse Books, 2019. ISBN 9781909031883.

Quast, Bruno, *Vom Kult zur Kunst. Öffnungen des Rituellen Textes in Mittelalter und Früher Neuzeit.* **Bibliotheca Germanica** 48. Tübingen, Francke A Verlag, 2005. ISBN 9783772080197.

Rodebaugh, Thomas L, *The Face of Evil*. **The Black Archive** #27. Edinburgh, Obverse Books, 2019. ISBN 9781909031791.

Rollason, Jane, *Doctor Who: The Girl Who Died*. **Pearson English Graded Readers Level 2**. London, Pearson Education, 2018. ISBN 9781292206134.

Salisbury, Joyce E, ed, *Sex in the Middle Ages: A Book of Essays*. 1991. New York/London, Garland, 2019. ISBN 9780367031022.

Jochens, Jenny, 'Before the Male Gaze: The Absence of the Female Body in Old Norse', pp3-29.

Sandifer, Elizabeth, *Volume 3: Jon Pertwee*. **TARDIS Eruditorum: An Unofficial Critical History of Doctor Who**. Ithaca, Eruditorum Press, 2018. ISBN 9781791574963.

Sandifer, Elizabeth, *Volume 4: Tom Baker and the Hinchcliffe Years*. **TARDIS Eruditorum: An Unofficial Critical History of Doctor Who**. Ithaca, Eruditorum Press, 2019. ISBN 9781078480666.

Sandifer, Elizabeth, *Volume 6: Peter Davison & Colin Baker*. **TARDIS Eruditorum: An Unofficial Critical History of Doctor Who**. Ithaca, Eruditorum Press, 2020. ISBN 9798645736552.

von Schnurbein, Stefanie, *Norse Revival: Transformations of German Neopaganism*. **Studies in Critical Research on Religion** Volume 5. Leiden/Boston, Brill, 2016. ISBN 9789004309517.

Skylitzes, John, *A Synopsis of Byzantine History, 811-1057*. Late 11th century. John Wortley, trans, Cambridge, Cambridge University Press, 2010. ISBN 9780521767057.

Snorri Sturluson, *Edda: Prologue and Gylfaginning*. c1220. Anthony Faulkes, trans, London, Everyman's Library, 2008. ISBN 9780460876162.

Snorri Sturluson, *The Prose Edda*. c.1220. Jesse L Byock, trans, Penguin Classics, 2005. ISBN 9780140447552.

Snorri Sturluson, *Heimskringla: Volume 1 – The Beginnings to Óláfr Tryggvason*. c1230. Anthony Faulkes and Alison Finlay, trans, London, Viking Society for Northern Research, 2016. ISBN 9780903521949.

Stott, Andrew, *Comedy*. **The New Critical Idiom**. Abingdon, Routledge, 2005. ISBN 9780415299336.

Svensson, Patrik, *The Gospel of the Eels: A Father, a Son and the World's Most Enigmatic Fish*, 2019. Agnes Broomé, trans, London, Picador/Pan Macmillan, 2020. ISBN 9781529030709.

Tolkien, JRR, *The Hobbit*. 1937. London, the Folio Society, 2002. ISBN 9785329002676.

Tolkien, JRR, *The Lord of the Rings*. 1954-55. New York, HarperCollins, 2003. ISBN 9780007172009.

Tulloch, John, and Manuel Alvarado, *Doctor Who: The Unfolding Text*. London, Palgrave Macmillan, 1983. ISBN 9780333348482.

Turville-Petre, Gabriel, *Nine Norse Studies*. London, Viking Society for Northern Research, 1972. ISBN 9780903521055.

Wells, HG, *The War of the Worlds*. 1892. London, Heinemann Educational Books, 1968. ISBN 9780435120054.

Wikström af Edholm, Klas, Peter Jackson Rova, Andreas Nordberg, Olof Sundqvist, and Torun Zachrisson, eds, *Myth, Materiality and Lived Religion: In Merovingian and Viking Scandinavia*. Stockholm, Stockholm University Press, 2019. ISBN 9789176350973.

Kuusela, Tommy, 'Halls, Gods and Giants: The Enigma of Gullveig in Óðinn's Hall', pp25-57.

Wilkinson, Joy, *The Witchfinders*. **The Target Doctor Who Library**. London, BBC Books, 2021. ISBN 9781785945021.

Periodicals

Doctor Who Magazine (DWM), Marvel UK, Panini, 1979-.

Arnopp, Jason, 'Episode Preview: *The Girl Who Died*'. DWM #492, cover date December 2015.

Arnopp, Jason, 'Immortal Words: The 2015 Team! Jamie Mathieson'. DWM #493, cover date Winter 2015/16.

Kibble-White, Graham, 'The DWM Review: *The Girl Who Died*'. DWM #493, cover date Winter 2015/16.

Rayner, Jacqueline, 'Relative Dimensions: Girl, Resurrected'. DWM #493, cover date Winter 2015/16.

Reveille, IPC Newspapers Ltd, 1940-79. Issue cover dated January 7-13, 1965.

'Spaceman Bill is Down to Earth'.

postmedieval: a journal of medieval cultural studies, Palgrave Macmillan, 2010-. 5:2 'Comic Medievalism', 2014.

D'Arcens, Louise, 'Medievalist Laughter', pp116-25.

Matthews, David, 'Said in Jest: Who's Laughing at the Middle Ages (and When)?', pp126-39.

Ainsworth, John, ed, ***Doctor Who****: The Complete History Volume 81: Under the Lake / Before the Flood / The Girl Who Died*. Panini UK Ltd, 2018.

Auld, Richard L, 'The Psychological and Mythic Unity of the God, Óðinn'. *Numen: International Review for the History of Religions* 23, 1976, Brill, pp145-60.

Ármann Jakobsson, 'The Trollish Acts of Þorgrímr the Witch: The Meanings of *Troll* and *Ergi* in Medieval Iceland'. *Saga-Book* XXXII, 2008, Viking Society for Northern Research, pp39-68.

Bala, Michael, 'The Clown: An Archetypal Self-Journey'. *Jung Journal: Culture and Psyche* 4:1, 2010, Taylor & Francis, pp50-71.

Charles, Alec, 'Three Characters in Search of an Archetype: Aspects of the Trickster and the *Flâneur* in the Characterizations of Sherlock Holmes, Gregory House, and Doctor Who'. *Journal of Popular Television* 1:1, 2013, Intellect Books, pp83-102.

Clover, Carol J, 'Regardless of Sex: Men, Women and Power in Early Northern Europe'. *Speculum* 68:2, 1993, University of Chicago Press, pp363-87.

Gardeła, Leszek, '"Warrior-Women" in Viking Age Scandinavia? A Preliminary Archaeological Study'. *Analecta Archaeologica Ressoviensia* 8, 2013, University of Rzeszów Press, pp273-340.

Hedenstierna-Jonson, Charlotte, Anna Kjellström, Torun Zachrisson, Maja Krzewińska, Veronica Sabrado, Neil Price, Torsten Günther, Mattias Jakobsson, Anders Götherström and Jan Storå, 'A Female Viking Warrior Confirmed by Genetics'. *American Journal of Physical Anthropology* 164:4, 2017, Wiley Periodicals, pp853-60.

Hodge, James L, '*New Bottles – Old Wine:* The Persistence of the Heroic Figure in the Mythology of Television Science Fiction and Fantasy'. *Journal of Popular Culture* 21:4, 1988, Wiley-Blackwell, pp37-48.

Motz, Lotte, 'Gullveig's Ordeal. A New Interpretation'. *Arkiv för Nordisk Filologi* 108, 1993, Lund University, pp80–92.

O'Connor, Ralph, 'History or Fiction? Truth-Claims and Defensive Narrators in Icelandic Romance-Sagas'. *Mediaeval Scandinavia* 15, 2005, Odense University Press, pp101-69.

Proyer, René T, 'A new Structural Model for the Study of Adult Playfulness: Assessment and Exploration of an Understudied Individual Differences Variable'. *Personality and Individual*

Differences 108, 2017, Elsevier, pp113-22.

Raffield, Ben, 'Playing Vikings: Militarism, Hegemonic Masculinities, and Childhood Enculturation in Viking Age Scandinavia'. *Current Anthropology* 60:6, 2019, University of Chicago Press, pp813-35.

Self, Kathleen M, 'The Valkyrie's Gender: Old Norse Shield-Maidens and Valkyries as a Third Gender'. *Feminist Formations* 26:1, 2014, Johns Hopkins University Press, pp143-72.

Solli, Brit, 'Queering the Cosmology of the Vikings: A Queer Analysis of the Cult of Odin and "Holy White Stones"'. *Journal of Homosexuality* 54:1/2, 2008, Routledge, pp192-208.

Television

Cyberbully, Raw TV, Channel 4, 2015.

Dad's Army, BBC, 1968-77.

Doctor Who, BBC, 1963-.

Game of Thrones, HBO, 2011-19.

MacGyver, Paramount Network Television, CBS Media Ventures, 1985-92, 2016-2021.

Monty Python's Flying Circus, BBC, 1969-74.

Noggin the Nog, BBC, 1959-65, 1982.

Norsemen/Vikingane, NRK, 2016-20.

The A-Team, Universal Television, NBC, 1983-87.

The Benny Hill Show, BBC, Associated Television, Thames Television, 1955-89.

The Last Kingdom, Carnival Film and Television, 2015-22.

The Lord of the Rings: The Rings of Power, Amazon Studios, New Line Cinema, 2022-.

The Mighty Boosh, Baby Cow Productions, 2004-7.

Eels, 2007.

Stargate SG-1, MGM Television, Double Secret Productions, Gekko Film Corp, Sony Pictures Television, Showtime Networks, Sci-Fi Originals, 1997-2007.

Vikings, TM Productions, Take 5 Productions, Octagon Films, Shaw Media, Corus Entertainment, MGM Television, 2013-20.

Rite of Passage, 2013.

Vikings: Valhalla, MGM Television, 2022.

Ways of Seeing, BBC, 1972.

Film

Bazalgette, Ed, dir, *The Last Kingdom: Seven Kings Must Die*. Carnival Film and Television, 2023.

Branagh, Kenneth, dir, *Thor*. Marvel Studios, Walt Disney Studios Motion Pictures, 2011.

Corman, Roger, dir, *The Saga of the Viking Women and their Voyage to the Waters of the Great Sea Serpent*. Malibu Productions, American International Pictures, 1958.

Eggers, Robert, dir, *The Northman*. Regency Enterprises, 2022.

Fleischer, Richard, dir, *The Vikings*. Bavaria Film, Brynaprod SA, Curtleigh Productions, 1958.

Gilliam, Terry, and Terry Jones, dir, *Monty Python and the Holy Grail*. Python (Monty) Pictures, 1975.

Jackson, Peter, dir, *The Hobbit: An Unexpected Journey*. Warner Bros. Pictures, New Line Cinema, Metro-Goldwyn-Mayer, WingNut Films, 2012.

Jackson, Peter, dir, *The Hobbit: The Desolation of Smaug*. Warner Bros. Pictures, New Line Cinema, Metro-Goldwyn-Mayer, WingNut Films, 2013.

Jackson, Peter, dir, *The Hobbit: The Battle of the Five Armies*. Warner Bros. Pictures, New Line Cinema, Metro-Goldwyn-Mayer, WingNut Films, 2014.

Jackson, Peter, dir, *The Lord of the Rings: The Fellowship of the Ring*. New Line Cinema, WingNut Films, 2001.

Jackson, Peter, dir, *The Lord of the Rings: The Two Towers*. New Line Cinema, WingNut Films, 2002.

Jackson, Peter, dir, *The Lord of the Rings: The Return of the King*. New Line Cinema, WingNut Films, 2003.

Jones, Terry, dir, *Erik the Viking*. Prominent Features, Svensk Filmindustri, 1989.

Jones, Terry, dir, *Monty Python's The Meaning of Life*. Celandine Films, The Monty Python Partnership, 1983.

Kurosawa, Akira, dir, *Seven Samurai*. Toho, 1954.

Miller, George, dir, *Mad Max: Fury Road*. Village Roadshow Pictures, Kennedy Miller Mitchell, RatPac-Dune Entertainment, 2015.

Neill, Roy William, dir, *The Viking*. Loew's Incorporated, Technicolor Motion Picture Corporation, Tec-Art Studios, Metro-Goldwyn-Mayer, 1928.

Pierce, Charles B, dir, *The Norseman*. Charles B Pierce Film Productions, Fawcett-Majors Productions, 1978.

Sturges, John, dir, *The Magnificent Seven*. The Mirisch Company, Alpha Productions, 1960.

Taylor, Alan, dir, *Thor: The Dark World*. Marvel Studios, Walt Disney Studios Motion Pictures, 2013.

Waititi, Taika, dir, *Thor: Ragnarok*. Marvel Studios, Walt Disney Studios Motion Pictures, 2017.

Waititi, Taika, dir, *Thor: Love and Thunder*. Marvel Studios, Walt Disney Studios Motion Pictures, 2022.

Zinnemann, Fred, dir, *High Noon*. Stanley Kramer Productions, United Artists, 1952.

Opera

Wagner, Richard, *Der Ring des Nibelungen* (*The Ring of the Nibelung*). WWV 86, 1848-74.

Das Rheingold (*The Rhinegold*). WWV 86A, premiere 1869.

Die Walküre (*The Valkyrie*). WWV 86B, premiere 1870.

Siegfried. WWV 86C, premiere 1876.

Götterdämmerung (*Twilight of the Gods*). WWV 86D, premiere 1876.

Gaming

The Lost Vikings. Silicon & Synapse (Blizzard Entertainment), Interplay Productions, 1993.

Web

[All links accessed 5 August 2022.]

Acker, Lizzy, 'Jeremy Christian's Vocabulary and Related Ideas, Explained'. *OregonLive*, 10 June 2017. https://www.oregonlive.com/portland/2017/06/jeremy_christians_vocabulary_a.html.

Alston, Trey, 'On **Game of Thrones**, No One was Safe – Now Everyone Is'. 5 January 2019. http://www.mtv.com/news/3122641/game-of-thrones-too-safe-season-8/.

BBC **Doctor Who**, Instagram post, 12 January 2016. https://www.instagram.com/p/BAclJ2yDqem/?utm_source=ig_web_copy_link.

BBC **Doctor Who**, Instagram post, 14 January 2016. https://www.instagram.com/p/BAg7ELvjqXc/?utm_source=ig_web_copy_link.

BBC Media Centre, '**Doctor Who** Reveals Maisie Williams as Guest Star'. 30 March 2015. https://www.bbc.co.uk/mediacentre/latestnews/2015/dw-maisie-williams.

BBC News, 'Erdogan poem: Turkey Demands German Action Over "Obscene" Satirist'. 11 April 2016. https://www.bbc.co.uk/news/world-europe-36013191.

BBC News, 'Jacob Zuma Painting: ANC to Sue South Africa's Brett Murray'. 18 May 2012. https://www.bbc.co.uk/news/world-africa-18115724.

BBC News, 'Kremlin Pulls Strings on TV Puppets'. 5 June 2000. http://news.bbc.co.uk/1/hi/world/monitoring/media_reports/778078.stm.

Beautiful Trouble, 'Clandestine Insurgent Rebel Clown Army'. https://beautifultrouble.org/toolbox/tool/clandestine-insurgent-rebel-clown-army/.

Birkett, Tom, 'US Capitol Riot: The Myths Behind the Tattoos Worn by "QAnon Shaman" Jake Angeli'. *The Conversation*, 11 January 2021. https://theconversation.com/us-capitol-riot-the-myths-behind-the-tattoos-worn-by-qanon-shaman-jake-angeli-152996.

Birkett, Tom, 'Why Far-Right Extremists Co-opt Norse Symbolism'. *The Week*, 20 June 2022. https://www.theweek.co.uk/news/crime/957122/why-far-right-extremists-co-opt-norse-symbolism.

Bruney, Gabrielle, '**Game of Thrones**'s Treatment of Women Will Tarnish Its Legacy'. *Esquire*, 11 April 2019. https://www.esquire.com/entertainment/tv/a27099255/game-of-thrones-treatment-of-women-controversy-legacy/.

Campbell, Jane, 'The Eyes Have It (**Doctor Who:** *The Girl Who Died*)'. 20 October 2015. http://www.eruditorumpress.com/blog/the-eyes-have-it-doctor-who-the-girl-who-died/.

Carless, Will, 'An Ancient Nordic Religion is Inspiring White Supremacist Terror'. *RevealNews,* 25 May 2017.

https://revealnews.org/article/an-ancient-nordic-religion-is-inspiring-white-supremacist-jihad/.

Carr, Mary Kate, 'Maisie Williams Was "Surprised" by That **Game of Thrones** Sex Scene – Because She Thought Arya Was Queer'. *AVClub*, 15 June 2022. https://www.avclub.com/maisie-williams-game-of-thrones-sex-scene-arya-stark-qu-1849065155.

Colwill, Lee, 'The King's Two Bodies? *Snjáskvæði* and the Performance of Gender'. University of Iceland, 4 May 2018. http://hdl.handle.net/1946/29928.

Cooijmans, Christian, 'Beyond Hostility and Hypermasculinity: Why We Need to Think Differently About the Vikings'. *HistoryExtra*, 16 April 2022. https://www.historyextra.com/period/viking/vikings-hostility-hypermasculinity-opinion/.

Dale, Roderick, 'It's Reigning Men: The Use and Abuse of Viking Masculinity'. 8 May 2019. https://roderickdale.co.uk/2019/05/08/its-reigning-men-the-use-and-abuse-of-viking-masculinity/.

Dearden, Lizzie, 'New Zealand Attack: How Nonsensical White Genocide Conspiracy Theory Cited by Alleged Gunman is Spreading Poison Around the World'. *The Independent*, 16 March 2019. https://www.independent.co.uk/news/world/australasia/new-zealand-christchurch-mosque-attack-white-genocide-conspiracy-theory-a8824671.html.

Edwards, Catherine, 'We Can't Let Racists Redefine Viking Culture'. *The Local*, 6 October 2017. https://www.thelocal.se/20171006/we-cant-let-racists-re-define-viking-culture-far-right-runes-swedish/.

Elledge, Jonn, Tweet posted on 21 March 2022.

https://twitter.com/JonnElledge/status/1506042667003752453.

Eva Dagbjört Óladóttir, 'The Privilege of Pain: "Manpain" and the Suffering Hero in the **Supernatural** Series'. Bachelor's dissertation at the University of Iceland, Skemman.is, 16 January 2014. https://skemman.is/bitstream/1946/17153/1/BAritgEvaO%cc%81lado%cc%81ttir.pdf.

Ferguson, Craig, 'The Lost **Doctor Who** Cold Open'. YouTube, 1 December 2010. https://www.youtube.com/watch?v=M9P4SxtphJ4.

Fontaine, Andie Sophia, 'Pagan Chief Says Racists Co-opt Elements of Ásátru'. *The Reykjavík Grapevine*, 28 August 2014. https://grapevine.is/news/2014/08/28/pagan-chief-says-racists-co-opt-elements-of-asatru/.

Graham, Jack, 'A Surfeit of Lampreys'. 23 October 2015. http://www.eruditorumpress.com/blog/a-surfeit-of-lampreys/.

Harper, Daniel, and Jack Graham, *I Don't Speak German*. 2019-. https://idontspeakgerman.libsyn.com/.

Hassell, Clint, '*The Girl Who Died* Review'. *DoctorWhoTV*, 18 October 2015. https://www.doctorwhotv.co.uk/the-girl-who-died-review-77069.htm.

Heimbuch, Jaymi, '8 Shocking Facts About Electric Eels'. *Treehugger*, 3 April 2022. https://www.treehugger.com/shocking-facts-about-electric-eels-4863966.

Holmes, Jonathan, 'Was This a Shocking Plot Hole in **Doctor Who**: *The Girl Who Died*?' *Radio Times*, 17 October 2015. http://web.archive.org/web/20151018141907/https://www.radiot

imes.com/news/2015-10-17/was-this-a-shocking-plot-hole-in-doctor-who-the-girl-who-died/.

Jeffery, Morgan, '**Game of Thrones** Exec: "No-one is Safe"'. *DigitalSpy*, 17 Feb 2011.https://www.digitalspy.com/tv/ustv/a304366/game-of-thrones-exec-no-one-is-safe/.

Kashevsky, Max, 'Folk Heroes and the Doctor: **Doctor Who**'s "Mythological Celebrity" Stories'. *Tor*, 25 June 2020. https://www.tor.com/2020/06/25/folk-heroes-and-the-doctor-doctor-whos-mythological-celebrity-stories/.

Kim, Dorothy, 'White Supremacists Have Weaponized an Imaginary Viking Past. It's Time to Reclaim the Real History'. *Time*, 12 April 2019. https://time.com/5569399/viking-history-white-nationalists/.

Lawler, Kelly, 'From Ricky Gervais to Dave Chappelle, Netflix has a Trans-Bashing Comedy Problem'. *USAToday*, 24 May 2022. https://eu.usatoday.com/story/entertainment/tv/2022/05/24/gervais-chappelle-netflix-has-trans-bashing-comedy-problem/9908713002/.

Martyn-Hemphill, Richard, and Henrik Pryser Libell, 'Who Owns the Nazis? Pagans, Neo-Nazis and Advertisers Tussle over Symbols'. *New York Times*, 17 March 2018. https://www.nytimes.com/2018/03/17/world/europe/vikings-sweden-paganism-neonazis.html.

Moffat, Steven, 'Hell Bent', 17 August 2015 draft, BBC Writers' Room. https://www.bbc.co.uk/writersroom/scripts/tv-drama/doctor-who.

Moffat, Steven, Instagram comment, 14 September 2021.

https://www.instagram.com/p/CTy1jXdsT6k/c/17933419039657896/r/17922153580870623/.

Mooney, Darren, '**Doctor Who**: *The Girl Who Died* (Review)'. *TheM0vieBlog*, 18 October 2015. https://them0vieblog.com/2015/10/18/doctor-who-the-girl-who-died-review/.

Mulkern, Patrick, '**Doctor Who**: *The Girl Who Died*'. *Radio Times*, 17 October 2015. https://www.radiotimes.com/tv/sci-fi/doctor-who-guide/the-girl-who-died/.

Price, Neil, 'What Stereotypes About Viking Masculinity Get Wrong'. *Time*, 25 August 2020. https://www.time.com/5882287/viking-gender/.

Price, Neil, 'Unpacking the Viking Caricature of Masculinity'. 20 August 2020. https://www.penguin.co.uk/articles/2020/august/children-ash-elm-neil-price-viking-gender-masculinity.html.

Reuters Health, 'Most Steroid Users are Not Athletes: Study'. Reuters, 21 November 2007. https://www.reuters.com/article/us-steroid-users-idUSCOL17558920071121.

Rose City Antifa, 'The Wolves of Vinland: A Fascist Countercultural "Tribe" in the Pacific Northwest'. 7 November 2016. https://rosecityantifa.org/articles/the-wolves-of-vinland-a-fascist-countercultural-tribe-in-the-pacific-northwest/.

Rose, Steve, 'Norse Code: Are White Supremacists Reading Too Much Into *The Northman*?' *The Guardian*, 22 April 2022. https://www.theguardian.com/film/2022/apr/22/norse-code-white-supremacists-reading-the-northman-robert-eggers.

Sandifer, Elizabeth, 'Brave Viking Warriors Slain by the Curse (*The Girl Who Died*)'. 23 July 2018. http://www.eruditorumpress.com/blog/brave-viking-warriors-slain-by-the-curse-the-girl-who-died/.

Sandifer, Elizabeth, 'Doing Better About Nazis'. 13 November 2019. https://www.freyjaskiss.com/doing-better-about-nazis/.

Sandifer, Elizabeth, 'Make Me a Warrior Now (*A Good Man Goes to War*)'. 28 April 2014. https://www.eruditorumpress.com/blog/make-me-a-warrior-now-a-good-man-goes-to-war.

Sandifer, Elizabeth, 'Time Can Be Rewritten: "Night of the Doctor"'. 28 July 2015. https://www.eruditorumpress.com/blog/time-can-be-rewritten-night-of-the-doctor.

Seyfried, Stewart, '**Doctor Who** – Series 9 Deleted Scene – *The Girl Who Died*'. *YouTube*, 7 August 2017. https://www.youtube.com/watch?v=Zxqo6FplmYc&t=3s.

Simone, Gail, 'Women in Refrigerators'. March 1999. https://www.lby3.com/wir/.

Smith, SE, '**Game of Thrones**' Fantasy Misogyny'. *Global Comment*, 1 June 2014. https://globalcomment.com/game-of-thrones-fantasy-misogyny/.

Sommer, Will, 'How "Soy Boy" Became the Far Right's Favorite New Insult'. *Medium*, 26 October 2017. https://medium.com/@willsommer/how-soy-boy-became-the-far-rights-favorite-new-insult-e2e988d365c7.

Trafford, Simon, 'Hyper-Masculinity vs Viking warrior-Women: Pop

Culture Vikings and Gender'. 11 January 2019. https://blogg.mah.se/historiskastudier/2019/01/11/hyper-masculinity-vs-viking-warrior-women-pop-culture-vikings-and-gender/.

Warner, Terry, '**Doctor Who**: 10 Special Effects That Totally Sucked'. *WhatCulture*, 25 May 2015. https://whatculture.com/tv/doctor-who-10-special-effects-that-totally-sucked.

Weber, Shannon, 'White Supremacy's Old Gods: The Far Right and Neopaganism'. 1 February 2018. https://www.politicalresearch.org /2018/02/01/white-supremacys-old-gods-the-far-right-and-neopaganism.

Wiggins, Anna, 'Guest Post: Odin and the Doctor'. September 2012. http://www.eruditorumpress.com/blog/guest-post-odin-and-the-doctor/.

Wilkins, Alasdair, 'Go watch tonight's *Doctor Who* right now, please and thank you'. *The AV Club,* 17 October 2015. https://tv.avclub.com/go-watch-tonight-s-doctor-who-right-now-please-and-tha-1798185405.

Wilson, Jason, 'Eco-Fascism is Undergoing a Revival in the Fetid Culture of the Extreme Right'. *The Guardian*, 19 March 2019. https://www.theguardian.com/world/commentisfree/2019/mar/20/eco-fascism-is-undergoing-a-revival-in-the-fetid-culture-of-the-extreme-right.

Woolf, Alex, 'Goodbye to the Vikings'. *History Today* 72:6, June 2022. https://www.historytoday.com/archive/behind-times/goodbye-vikings.

ACKNOWLEDGEMENTS

I first had the idea (and, indeed, outlined the general structure) for this book way back in 2017, so it has been brewing for a long time. On the many stopping points in that journey, a number of people have provided guidance, advice, and sensitivity reading of various passages: I would like to thank (in no particular order) Evan Jones, Max Kashevsky, Jon Arnold, Becky Cummings, Lee Colwill, Jonathan Dennis, Brendan O'Shea, Andrew Davies, Christa Mactíre, Aristide Twain, Moon J Cobwebb, Nicks Walker, Thomas Keyton, Cameron Joshua, Richard O'Hagan, Jack Graham, Matthew Clark, Chris Lees, and Usha Vishnuvajjala. I owe a great debt to various tutors who inspired and/or cultivated my love of medievalism and Norse mythology – Annette Volfing, Henrike Lähnemann, Heather O'Donoghue, and Judy Quinn; needless to say, this book would never have come into existence without their academic guidance. In **Doctor Who** terms, this book similarly would not exist without Elizabeth Sandifer paving the way in terms of her extensive critical analysis of the programme. My various editors over the years have also been of great help in terms of honing my writing and so I am indebted to them all – especially the editors of this range, Philip Purser-Hallard and Paul Driscoll, who have done such sterling work both on my manuscript and on the range in general. Lastly, thanks to my parents and to Simon for their baffled-but-proud support (especially my Dad for sourcing a book from the University of Bern Library), and of course, all my thanks and love to Joanna, as always.

BIOGRAPHY

Tom Marshall holds a BA in German Language and Literature from the University of Oxford and an MPhil in Anglo-Saxon, Norse, and Celtic from the University of Cambridge, specialising in ecocritical readings of Ragnarǫk; he is also a member of the Viking Society for Northern Research. He now works as a freelance copyeditor, proofreader, translator, and private tutor based in Cumbria. He has written about **Doctor Who** in various publications since the age of 15, including examinations of *The Rescue* and *Mummy on the Orient Express* in two volumes of *Outside In*, a study of the BBCi *Shada* in *You and 42: The Hitchhiker's Guide to Douglas Adams*, contributing assessments of five stories to *Army of Ghosts: Essays About Doctor Who's Sometimes Forgotten Stories*, as well as contributions to *DWRG* and *CultBox*. Outside of **Doctor Who,** he has also been published on topics such as the BBC's adaptation of *Jonathan Strange & Mr Norrell,* David Bowie's 1977 single 'Heroes', and, for the online journal *New Voices in Translation*, Ulrike Draesner's bilingual novel about the life of Kurt Schwitters. His translation of Draesner's essay 'Huhediblu' appears in the de Gruyter Companion to the poet Paul Celan. Most recently, he has started co-hosting (with Kevin Burnard) the podcast **K9: BingeQuake** (@K9BingeQuake on Twitter), delving into the unloved and unwatched Australian **K9** TV series, episode by episode; he's still not quite sure why they're doing this.